HANG ONTO
THE WILLOWS

By

ERNESTINE GRAVLEY

★

Pen Drawings
by
AUGUSTA I. C. METCALFE

BISON PRESS
Shawnee, Oklahoma
1957

FOREWORD

This book is essentially an authentic story of the life and experiences of a colorful, pioneer doctor who staked his claim at the turn of the century in the little town of Grand, Oklahoma Territory, county seat of old Day county, which was abolished by the statehood of Oklahoma in 1907 to become a part of present day Ellis county.

After he became highly successful, Dr. O. C. Newman, subject of this story was asked what period of his life he treasured most. His prompt reply was "Territorial days."

Here, in old Day county, the treacherous South Canadian river was to him a constant challenge with its raging floods, tricky quicksand bars and breaks through the ice in winter, when he called on his patients by horseback or buggy. A man of less courage and determination could not have braved the deprivation and suffering of a raw, new frontier, to become a legend. But, as a pioneer of old Grand observed, it was because he stuck it out and hung onto the willows, that O. C. Newman became great. It was from this colorful and significant statement that the author took her title for this work.

I consider Ernestine Gravley a most excellent writer, sympathetic with the material she handles, and technically quite competent as well as capable of giving creative imagination to her work.

John Wesley Raley, President
Oklahoma Baptist University

Contents

INTRODUCTION

For many years, it has seemed to me that a great and purposeful life such as that of Dr. O. C. Newman should not be kept only in the memories of those who knew him personally, but shared with all people who could appreciate the personal sacrifice he made to remain with his own people as a country doctor.

So it was that I conceived an idea. I wrote scores of letters, made hundreds of phone calls and traveled extensively to gather bits of data, unassembled notes and spoken words of colorful memory to add to the growing accumulation of material for this book.

HANG ONTO THE WILLOWS is written with skill and sensitive understanding by Ernestine Gravley, whose work was recommended to the Newman family and to me by Dr. John Wesley Raley, president of Oklahoma Baptist University and by five members of that faculty. As the work progressed, it has been my growing conviction that Divine Guidance led us to the author.

Augusta I. C. Metcalfe, the artist whose clever, clean-cut pen drawings illustrate this volume, is a long-time friend of the Newman family; a person who knew and admired the doctor. A true pioneer, Mrs. Metcalfe is a native daughter of the Panhandle country so graphically portrayed in this true life story.

Frances Pior Tubb

Dr. O. C. Newman
1876-1953

CHAPTER I

A Boy Dreams

*". . . All through the prairie countries
and out across the plains to the passes
of the Rockies there are people who have
reason to bless the name of Dr. Newman."*

Far up the winding road, the wheels of Dr.
Berry's sturdy old buggy rattled over the stones.
Oscar could hear the exciting sound from his private
lookout near the creek. The ten-year-old boy, leaning on his hoe handle in the tobacco patch, looked
around quickly. Doctor was going on another call!

The year was 1886 and the settlement was yet
sparse around Jaybird, Ohio. Like other farmers
of Adams county, Oscar's father was substantially
settled and though not wealthy, the large family
was always comfortable.

Mesheck Herdman Newman, father of ten
children of whom Oscar was the next to youngest,
instilled deeply into five sons and five daughters
a strong sense of independence. This character trait
was manifest in Oscar Newman from boyhood
throughout his life.

The fine Newman farm was well supplied with
help, for in addition to the immediate family, four
grandchildren and a nephew shared bed and board.
The girls were handy at helping around the house
at cooking, canning, grinding coffee, sewing and
quilting.

Oscar's mother, the gentle Sarah was never idle. When she found time to sit by the log fire on long winter evenings, the mending basket was always at hand; her patient fingers darning homespun stockings and patching the seats of innumerable pairs of britches. Oscar's twin brother, Edgar, usually a constant companion was puzzled when his twin chose to be alone in some corner with a book, or up near the creek bank in the opening of a plum thicket. At these times, Oscar was dreaming of the day when he would become a man and, like his ideal, Dr. Berry, a country doctor!

The buggy was coming closer now. Oscar's heart pounded wildly as the vehicle raced around the curve just before fording the creek. Doc was sitting very erect, his round black hat hardly covering the bushy hair that fringed out from the narrow brim. The same rusty black suit he had worn for several years looked dignified and correct to the small boy as he gazed admiringly at the wonderful sight. There on the seat beside Doctor was the black bag, holding in its depths the pills and other mysterious items for healing the sick.

Oscar waved to his good friend and called, "Hall-oo, Dr. Berry! How are you, sir?"

"Whoa," boomed Dr. Berry, pulling in on the reins as the horse stumbled to a halt. "Well, good morning, Oscar, and a nice spring morning it is."

"Yes, sir. Is somebody sick, sir?"

"Nigh to dyin', likely. Do they ever have the good sense to call on me early, when medicine would do the most good?" He shook his head sadly and clucked to the horse, which plunged across the shallow creek and headed in a trot toward Peach Mountain.

Still leaning on the hoe handle, Oscar watched him go. The tobacco patch was surrounded by lacy pine, majestic oak and walnut trees. Among them, wild plum trees bloomed riotously and a mass of bees hummed among the fluffy, white blossoms, but the boy paid no mind. He was thinking of Dr. James S. Berry, his ideal.

The boy had already inquired into the life of the man and learned that he had followed the tanner's trade of his father until the age of eighteen. Five years of school teaching was followed by medical school where he had graduated from Starling Medical College.

To Oscar, Dr. Berry was the perfect man. He was learned in legal matters, and many of the citizens of Adams county had called on him for counsel at one time or another. The doctor was temperate of habits, a lifelong abstainer from intoxicating liquor and tobacco. He was engaged in banking, farming, the sale of farming implements, the raising of stock and he gave much thought and energy to educational matters!

But perhaps the thing that endeared Dr. Berry most to the country boy was his sense of humor. Though sympathetic, he used among the sick his gift for story telling and it was commonly said that he could make a dying man laugh and be the better for it.

But it was true, what Doc had said about people neglecting to call early enough. Why, he could remember only a few times when the doctor had made a professional call at his house, though he was frequently there as a neighbor and friend. People only called a doctor as a last resort after home remedies failed to cure weeks of sickness. And always, sending for a physician meant an urgent plea to hurry.

Pap and Ma had a big, black doctor book on the clock shelf, along with the family Bible and a worn copy of Shakespeare. Taking down the doctor book and thumbing through its pages seemed a solemn rite when one of the family became ill or received an injury. On these occasions, Oscar's fingers itched to handle the awe-inspiring book with its authoritative instructions for home healing, but the answer to his earnest request was always the same: "Wait until you are older."

There was the time last summer when Oscar was cutting sorghum cane with a curved-blade hand scythe and the sharp point slashed into a vein of his foot. The scarlet blood had gushed onto the sand and when they had carried him to the square kitchen, Ma sat right down on the floor searching frantically through the doctor book for a way to stop the flow.

While Ma read the instructions to pack flour into the wound, Oscar's blood had gushed onto the page by his bare foot and sort of sealed the covenant he had made earlier to be a country doctor. Even with the big book closed there on the shelf, he could see the dark brown stain of his own blood along the edge of the page, like a proud badge.

Every family around Jaybird kept supplies of camphor, turpentine and mentholatum and not a

14 . . .

few youngsters were "protected" from the on-slaught of disease by a chunk of stinking assafoe-tida hanging on a string around his neck. Some of the boys at school carried a rabbit's foot to ward off sickness and all forms of bad luck, but the Newmans were never superstitious, as were some of their neighbors.

Oscar knew that a doctor should be educated and while other boys played pranks and avoided work in the old schoolhouse at Jaybird, he studious-ly pursued his schooling. The first year was spent on the ABC's, learning to recite them forward and backward, mastering the lettering in block, capital and small script on his slate. The following year, he took McGuffey's First Reader. While his class-mates read laboriously aloud in a monotonous and expressionless drone, Oscar's mind raced ahead. While the other scholars learned to pronounce the words of the First Reader, Oscar memorized whole sections of the book.

And now, at ten years old he had finished the Third Reader. The boy raised his head and sniffed at the plum boughs. It was good here in his private world with the sounds of Doc's buggy wheels dying in the distance, but they would be needing him at home. He slid down the high embankment and went whistling toward the farmhouse where a bountiful noon dinner waited. Maybe the family did think him a bit touched in the head for wanting to be a doctor, but some day they would understand and see he was right.

The ancestors of Oscar Clarence Newman were God-fearing, simple, law-abiding people, the des-cendants of Christopher Newman who was born in Virginia in 1769 and married Sarah Ross in the same state, going to Ohio in the year of 1799.

The pioneering couple settled on a farmstead in Scioto county in the southern part of the state. Here, they became the parents of a round dozen children, Oscar's grandfather, John Newman being the ninth of twelve. John was born in 1814 and at the age of twenty-four married Anna Herdman who was born in Germany in 1819 and came to Virginia at an early age. The Newman lineage was English and arrived in Virginia from England at least one generation before Christopher Newman.

John and Anna had ten children, the second of whom was Oscar's father, Mesheck Herdman Newman, born on September 18, 1840.

It was in the historic year of 1860 that he took Sarah Johnson as his bride, a soulful girl of Irish descent whose mother's maiden name was Scowden and came from the Emerald Isle. It was significant, with her Christ-like qualities that Sarah was born on Christmas Day, 1839.

Mesheck Herdman Newman had been born near Rardin, Adams county, Ohio and reared as a farmer. He received only a common school education, but was quite active in community affairs. He was a Justice of the Peace of Franklin Township from 1874 to 1877 and was later Treasurer of the Township for a year. Beginning on January 2, 1894, Mr. Newman was a County Commissioner of Adams county.

Mesheck and Sarah were parents of ten children and at the time of Oscar's birth, he of whom this biography is written, was the 623rd descendant from the marriage of Christopher Newman and Sarah Ross. The twin brother, Edgar was the eighth of ten children and Oscar was the ninth on that birth date, December 29, 1876.

Oscar kept alive his dream of becoming a country doctor during the three years following, while he mastered one by one the McGuffey's Fourth, Fifth and Sixth Readers. The homely philosophy within these much honored books stayed in the boy's mind and became a part of his own philosophy. Now that he had completed the Sixth Reader, he was, in the thinking of the humble people of Adams county, an advanced student.

The next move faced him with great challenge and not a little doubt. He was still far from a man and it would be asking quite a bit of his parents to send him to medical school. Oscar talked often and earnestly with them.

"Son, I think it's mighty fine and all that, your wanting to be a healer of the sick," his mother said one day, putting an arm about his shoulders. "But you have to make a living, too. Surely you know that these people have little or no money for the services of a doctor. Mostly, they just get along without such help."

"But can't you see?" Oscar exclaimed. "Ministering to the sick and dying should be only a part of what a doctor does for his people. Teaching them how to stay well is equally important."

His father cleared his throat loudly and said: "You have the right idea, Oscar, but getting folks to come around to your way of thinking is quite another thing. So long as there are home remedies and patent medicines and midwives, people hardly ever need a doctor."

"And when they do, it's often too late," Oscar said bitterly.

All that summer, as he went about the chores of the farm, helping to lay by the crops, cutting cords of firewood for the coming winter, the young man, now seventeen, pondered his problem. Late in August, he put his belongings in a battered old valise and started on foot to Peebles, Ohio, seven miles west of home.

Oscar's legs were young and strong and for much of the distance, he walked, with an occasional short lift from a mail hack or a passing farm wagon.

Peebles was a larger town than he had ever seen, and he approached the head of the Adams County Normal School with all the embarrassment of a country lad.

"And how do you plan to utilize the higher education you receive?" the headmaster asked.

"Sir, if I can pass examination and get a teacher's certificate, I hope to go back home and teach school, at least for a term or so."

The headmaster eyed him carefully. "Young man, if it is your desire to be an educator, why do you speak of only a term or so?"

Oscar looked down at his shoes which were covered with dust. What would this man say if he told the whole truth; that he wanted to teach only until he could save enough money for medical school without the aid of anyone? He raised his head and took a chance. "If I should discover that teaching is my life's calling, I'll continue in that field, sir. Meantime, I shall make the most possible of every opportunity in your school."

The headmaster smiled broadly and extended his hand. Here was a young fellow who would go places!

Oscar paid strict attention to his studies, for he dared not fail the examination. Invitations to most social events were of necessity declined, but Oscar's warm and forthright personality won for him many friends at Adams County Normal.

At full young manhood, Oscar Newman had reached the height of five feet, eleven inches. His eyes were a steady blue and his hair was light brown. His was an erect carriage which was often referred to as symbolic of his straight and noble character.

The following summer, Oscar was back home with a certificate to teach the home district school. It was good to be alive, surrounded by the abundant meadows and fields; the creek and the plum thickets so dear to his boyhood.

Stirrings of young manhood quickened his pleasure in the association of friends and all that summer, he was happy and relaxed, fishing in the clear, cold streams and riding horseback over the colorful Ohio countryside.

Feeling the need of dignity befitting his coming role as schoolmaster, Oscar began to grow a beard. He was of husky build and wide of shoulders. The young lassies of the community began to notice him and to muffle shy giggles behind their handkerchiefs. But Oscar Newman was not ready for romance, for the dream of ministering to the healing of people came first in his thinking that summer.

When the fall term began, the young man put aside even his dream from conscious thinking and gave his entire effort to the neighborhood youngsters in the school room. Some of the boys in McGuffey's Sixth Reader were as large and practically as old as the teacher, and it was inevitable that they had to determine whether or not they could bully their instructor.

The boys began right away to play marbles "for keeps" and young Newman told them to leave their marbles at home unless they could play without gambling. But the practice went on among the older boys in defiance of his orders. He gave them three days, then during the noon dinner hour walked up to the game. The fellows glanced up briefly and returned to their shooting.

"All right," the young teacher said, " if you prefer a man-to-man basis, we'll do it that way. If I can win your marbles, do you agree not to bring any more to school?"

One by one, they agreed. The game went past time to "take up books" and the scholars were delighted, but the teacher won the marbles. Thereafter, he was looked upon with the respect due him.

Immediately following the close of school, young Newman enrolled for the summer course in the Manchester Normal College of Adams County to qualify for further teaching. That summer of 1894 was unusually hot and sticky. In addition, Newman was carrying a heavy scholastic load, but despite the heat, he stuck doggedly to his tasks.

Late one Sunday afternoon, Oscar was sitting on the front door steps when his mother joined him. A black thunder cloud had boiled up in the west and the distant rumble promised at least a brief respite from the heat.

"I suppose you are going to get the school again, Son?" she asked.

"I could. But I've decided it might be well to go right through another term of study. I've saved enough to carry me along by working on the side. What do you think, Ma?"

"You've always had a level head on your shoulders, Oscar. I think that you'll decide the best thing."

They were silent for a time. A quick, cool breeze from the thunderhead scampered across the fields and meadows, whisked over the creek and fanned up against their faces. The woman put a workworn hand over the hand of her son. "Oscar, you still think about being a doctor, don't you?"

"Yes, I have the same old dream. And Ma, I suppose Pap would think it crazy if I told him, but I'm still going to practice medicine some of these days, and when I get my M.D., I'm going to whatever place seems to need a doctor most."

"You're a good teacher, Oscar, and you'll be a better doctor." Ma Sarah sighed deeply. "You go right on with your plans, Son. So long as you're honest, industrious and God-fearing, your father and I will have no call to worry about you."

That fall, Oscar Newman entered the National Normal University at Lebanon, Ohio, conducted by Professor Alfred Halbrook as president. Never before had he been so conscious of the need for

Young O. C. Newman, at age nineteen, just before he taught his last term of school at Mineral Springs Station before starting to medical school.

22 . . .

more good doctors to drive ignorance and super-
stition from the thinking of people.

Returning home in the spring, Oscar frequently went about the countryside on calls with his
doctor friend, now past middle age. The doctor
worried a great deal about what would happen to the
suffering folk in those parts when he was gone.
The nearest doctor was over in the direction of
Cherry Fork, but the people seemed not to be
greatly concerned.

Oscar Newman's last school teaching experiences came the following term, 1895-96 when he
taught the eight-month winter term at Mineral
Springs Station. He had purchased a bicycle and
when the weather was fine, he pedaled from home,
up the rocky slope and over Peach Mountain to
the school house.

Mineral Springs was at that time a thriving
resort town. Tourists came from far and near to
make use of the healing mineral waters; seven
kinds of medicinal minerals flowed from the earth
here.

The school itself was a notch above many
country schools in the area. Not many years previous, there were only subscription schools, where
the teacher would canvass the countryside, signing
up the scholars for a small sum, perhaps a dollar
or so a month. The early school houses had been
one-room, log affairs with a native stone fireplace
and split logs for seats, placed on wooden pegs.

Now, with a better building, including wooden
floor and factory made desks, the situation was
much improved. Much of the community life re-

volved around the school, and scholastic feats were hailed then as much as are athletic events today.

Oscar Newman stayed over for the weekly spelling matches every Friday evening, returning home late at night on his bicycle. People of the community lined up in two even rows and the teacher gave out words first to one side, then the other. Upon missing a word, the participant was seated.

Suspense mounted as fewer were left standing, and a victor indeed was the one remaining. Champion spellers enjoyed popularity as does a football hero today.

Dinner buckets, usually empty lard pails, were hung on a row of nails outside the schoolhouse, high enough to be safe from roving dogs. Inside was to be found home-cured ham and bacon, boiled eggs, biscuits, molasses cake and fried, dried fruit pies. Many was the time when Oscar swapped some pupil a chunk of hot-seasoned sausage for a baked sweet potato, one of his favorite foods.

Some scholars came from as far away as five or six miles and there was a hitching post for their horses. As for the teacher, it was sometimes easier to walk; for instance, when there was deep snow on the ground, than to ride the bicycle.

Taking a cue from difficulties of the previous term, young Newman brought into the school room on the first day an armload of "hickories" as a suggestion in favor of good behavior. In addition to McGuffey Readers (and he taught all six) Newman used the Webster's Blue Back Spellers and taught a course in elementary geography of the

United States. Scholars were required to do rapid and accurate ciphering on their slates.

At the noon hour, the schoolmaster joined in the all-out game of "scrub" or "base" and all returned to their studies with greater enthusiasm after the rough play.

At the close of the term, the young teacher closed the door on a brief but rewarding experience. One by one, he had seen his scholars and members of their families have serious bouts with illness, heard the crude home treatments and in all too many cases, excused the students for the sad occasion of fatalities. It was not at all unusual for newborns to die within weeks of birth and a great many were stillborn.

Oscar Newman's mind was made up. In as short a time as possible, he would prepare himself for healing physical ailments of the common man.

CHAPTER II

The Medical Student

There was no time to lose. Now that his goal was fully determined, the young man selected Fayette College in Fulton county, Ohio in the extreme northern part of the state. This was the greatest journey he had ever made, a distance of some 225 miles. His old Adams county home was just across the Ohio river from Kentucky.

Throughout the summer, Newman worked long hours, falling exhausted into bed late at night and rising early for a new start. Without taking a break of even a few days, he finished the term in September, 1897 and immediately entered the College of Medicine of the National Normal University at Lebanon, Ohio. In later years, he could recall little of his experiences during this period, inasmuch as every waking hour was devoted to gruelling study and examinations.

First year courses satisfactorily completed were: Descriptive Anatomy; Physiology; Materia Medica and Therapy; Chemistry (organic) and Chemistry (inorganic); Histology and Microscopy; Bacteriology and Hygiene. Laboratory courses the same year were an extension of all the above-named and including Toxicology and Urinalysis. While here, he belonged to the YMCA, where E. C. McDougle was president and A. W. Drushel was recording secretary.

In 1898, O. C. Newman boarded a train for Sewanee, Tennessee where he enrolled in the medical school of the University of the South. The two years spent at Sewanee were among the most memorable of a colorful life. Newman was as extremely sensitive to beauty on the one hand as to suffering on the other. No campus in America is, or has ever been more beautiful than that of the University of the South in the great Cumberland mountains, and Oscar Newman was extravagant in praise of these surroundings.

Almost upon arrival, he sent a letter to the editor of his hometown paper in Ohio, followed by another a few weeks later. These clippings have been carefully preserved in a family scrapbook, and follow here verbatim.

Sewanee, Tennessee
May 22, 1898

A few lines from the top of the Cumberland. I hope it will be accepted in the columns of your paper. I'm not accustomed to writing but hope to make them interesting enough that it will not appear tedious for friends who care to read a letter from the Buckeye who has recently come here for further preparations to become in the future a recognized M.D.

In my first letter I will briefly describe my trip, and in my next items, I hope to describe the locality and environment of this distant town in the forests of the Cumberland Mountains.

Starting from home Tuesday morning, May 17, arriving at Cincinnati, I hurried hastily to the Grand Central depot in order to catch the 11 p.m. train on the L. and N. which came by way of Louisville, Kentucky. On my way I was not amazed to find the southern part of Kentucky and the northern part of Tennessee hilly and rocky for I am accustomed to the hills of Adams county. But they are surpassed in height and roughness by the two mentioned states; through parts, though, they are beautiful and level.

After a pleasant trip, I arrived at Nashville at 8:20. I registered at the Tulare Hotel and next morning at 9:10 I was again on my journey, hoping for the destination. At 12 o'clock, I changed cars for my journey up the mountain slope, the distance being eight miles.

It is wonderful to imagine such curves, and how the road winds around the slope. I have heard the story of the engineer and conductor on the rear coach shaking hands around curves, but I never saw it so nearly demonstrated before. It is amazing how a train can be managed in ascending slopes of a vast mountain 3,000 feet high.

Were I a poet I would attempt to describe in verse the beautiful scenery in the valley one can see as one nears the mountain top, but I'm sure I would fail in the attempt, and for that reason shall consider it null.

I arrived at Sewanee at 1 p.m., procured a room and am now ready for actual business. I was somewhat disappointed not to find a larger city, but I would most earnestly insist it is just the place to meet all requirements of a medical student, for the surroundings of the campus itself are not so attractive as to lead his mind from his books.

Yours truly, OCN
Sewanee College
July 4, 1898

. . . 29

Sewanee is situated on an elevated plateau, a spur of the Cumberland mountains some 2,000 feet above the level of the sea and about one thousand feet above the surrounding valleys. The temperature even in the hot season is delightful and well adapted to the requirements of a summer school.

The plateau is abundantly supplied with pure, cold, freestone water which is conveyed by pipes to the University buildings. Sewanee, the seat of the university is situated on a branch of the Nashville, Chattanooga and St. Louis railroad, about eighty-seven miles south of Nashville and sixty-nine miles north of Chattanooga. It is not noted for its well arranged streets, laid in squares, shaded with maple or some other transplantable trees, nor other improvements that are seen in larger towns. Its houses are scattered over a space of one thousand acres and of an average distance from each other of one hundred yards or more.

As has been mentioned above, Sewanee is the seat of the University of the South and the population consists mainly of students. The medical department deserves special mention on account of the superior advantages it offers. It was founded in 1892 and since that time has increased rapidly in growth and is destined to rank among the foremost colleges of its kind in the south. It was the first school of the south to adopt in its organic law the higher literary requirements for matriculation and the three courses of lectures before graduation. The last graduating class was drawn from twenty-three different states, representing every section of the country.

The medical school is in strict accord with Southern medical associations requirements, looking to a higher and more perfect education. Like many other towns it has its disadvantages, such as on the Sabbath, seemingly secluded from the whole world as far as transportation is concerned, for no train ascends the mountain on that day. The stillness is broken only by cool, pleasant breezes which are never absent from the necessity of pleasure and makes it very pleasant indeed.

Having such a climate as mentioned above would make it very healthful and those who seek for a constitutional restorer at this place or somewhere similar, are fortunate enough to be in the midst of the most beautiful scenery nature can afford.

Just south of the outskirts of the little village may be seen Mt. Disappointment. Looking from this prominent peak, not at a far distance, can be seen another prominent bluff which has larger and more rugged rocks projecting from its edges and overhanging the base. Intervening the two bluffs is a small valley thickly covered with forests which presents a beautiful view of nature. Just west of town is Morgan's Steep. It too is a grand view of more than a hundred feet high of which the summit overhangs the base more so than the one abovementioned. Looking from the summit, some more than eight miles, into the valley can be seen the small town of Cowan, and to the left the winding railroad which ascends the mountain.

To the north is Green View, the most extensive and more beautiful than any of the preceding. Many meadows and fields of grain can be seen in the extensive valley, and the beautiful farms are presented to view as far as can be seen. There are many other sceneries more beautiful than can be described or imagination can comprehend.

Since the water is so pure, the air so pleasant and healthful, and the sceneries so grand, why then does it not meet the requirements for students of any profession or those who seek health and pleasure? For the environments are suitable to meet any wants.

Yours truly, OCN

The young medical student was assigned a room on the second floor of Van Cleve House for which he paid eighteen dollars a month for room and board. All the students in this building were young men studying medicine who could not afford to pay high prices for a fancy room.

At the edge of the mountain there was a crystal clear, cold, gushing stream leaping a dozen feet over a projecting cliff. It was here that most of the boys took their regular Saturday night bath.

32 . . .

A narrow hallway separated Oscar from a sincere Texas freshman. They met in the hall on their first day and the Ohio boy put out a friendly hand. "I'm Oscar C. Newman. Looks like we're neighbors here."

"I'm Everett S. Lain," the youth responded. "Come from down Texas way. This is all new to me, being my first year in medical school."

"First year is the hardest, they say, but I've yet to find out. I'm only a sophomore with a great deal to learn but if I can be of any help—"

"Thanks, very much," Lain said. "I appreciate that offer."

It became a regular habit for the two boys to study together each evening, and in later years, Everett S. Lain, eminent Oklahoma City skin specialist said: "Especially did I welcome the tendered assistance of the Ohio boy who had previously taken his freshman year in a medical college in his home state." The two boys learned on closer acquaintance that their backgrounds were very similiar; each had been reared on a farm, had had one or two years of college, received a teacher's certificate and had taught in a country school.

When a particularly knotty problem faced one or both, they took long walks over the green forests of the Cumberland. A pleasant spot never to be forgotten was the outdoor shower bath. At the edge of the mountain there was a crystal clear, cold, gushing stream leaping a dozen feet over a projecting cliff. It was here that most of the boys took their regular Saturday night bath.

Oscar Newman was as eager as the rest

of the students to learn more about surgery and it was with great enthusiasm that they were allowed to sit in on a surgical clinic and observe an actual major operation in progress. Here, it was learned that the internal anatomy of a dog is much like that of the human body.

One evening, the young men were studying as usual when another of the students burst into the room excitedly. "Our chance has come," he cried, pointing in the direction of the kitchen.

Oscar's breath came faster. A patient!

"I've been watching for that old dog," the student went on. "A stray hound raids our garbage cans every night. Wouldn't the cooks be happy if he had to take a rest for a few days?"

"Seems to me a good hound dog would deserve the best appendectomy possible," Oscar Newman observed, as he began putting in order his few surgical instruments.

Several of the fellows stood guard that night for the visitor, and one boy, handy with a rope, lassoed him when he put in an appearance. Two of the willing assistants chloroformed the animal and O. C. Newman successfully removed the dog's appendix.

34 . . .

Several of the fellows stood guard that night
for the visitor, and one boy, handy with a rope,
lassoed him when he put in an appearance. Two
of the willing assistants chloroformed the animal
and O. C. Newman thereupon successfully removed

*In the spring of 1899, Dr. A. M. Newman, youngest
brother of Oscar's father invited the young man to
come out and look at the Panhandle country for a
possible location to practice. The two are pictured here
together.*

the dog's appendix. In recalling the event many years later, Everett S. Lain said that "unfortunately, no animal hospital was available, so our 'patient' was necessarily turned loose without proper post-operative care, but this can be known as the first major operation performed by the man who was later to build one of the outstanding hospitals and clinics in the Southwest."

In the spring of 1899, young Newman received a long letter from his uncle, the youngest brother of his father, Dr. A. M. Newman, a practicing physician in Canadian, Texas. "I am inclined," he wrote, "to agree with the advice of Horace Greeley when he said 'Go west, young man.' Oscar, would you accept my invitation to journey into our fresh new country this summer? Once here, I believe you will agree that the opportunities for a young doctor are endless in the wide spaces of the West."

The young man bid his friends goodbye for a short while, and assuring his return to the university for the opening of the fall term, he set out for Canadian, Texas. His first impression as he crossed the plains of Oklahoma Territory and Indian Territory was a feeling of bleakness. It looked like everything but a likely place to settle and set up practice. He was frankly discouraged.

Nevertheless, it was delightful to see again the uncle whom he admired and they spent several weeks looking over the villages and small towns of the Texas panhandle and western Oklahoma. At a general store in Grand, Oklahoma, they "chewed the rag" with a group of settlers. All were garbed pretty much alike in the sturdy clothes of the pioneer.

"I homesteaded the year of the Run," said a bewhiskered, tall man with kindly eyes. "I've seen quite some floods on the old South Canadian these ten years."

"Dust is worse," spoke up another. "Personally, I've had no crops to get damaged, but my wife has had many a washing get ruined by the dust."

"It's a good country; I like it," said a third. "Folks are mighty friendly and helpful hereabout."

After the crowd had drifted out, young Newman asked the proprietor what those who spoke out did for a living.

"Well, let me see now. That was a conglomeration of folks. It sure was. The first was a rancher; came from New York state where he was in some line of insurance, I believe. And then the fellow whose wash gets dirty—he is setting up law practice and his pretty wife is from a family of high society back East. The last one was just a drifter; got no people, I take it. He's working at odd jobs for Andy Dunn east of here."

For the first time, Oscar was really impressed. Here were people of varying backgrounds and all parts of the United States, living together on an equal social status, carving a good life in a new and raw country. He could feel at ease among these people.

"Who is the doctor here?" Oscar asked the proprietor.

The man looked surprised. "I reckon a doctor would be a luxury in Grand. Nope, there's no doctor in all of Day county, for that matter. Sure

. . . 37

O. C. Newman on the day he received his degree of
Doctor of Medicine from the University of the South
at Sewanee, Tennessee.

38 . . .

would be fine, though. Put our women folk's minds at ease."

Oscar looked at Uncle Alfred, who was studying him intently. He suddenly remembered his mother beside him on the front steps at home and a summer shower coming up. "I stake my claim as a citizen of Grand," the young man declared. "Next year, I'll be back with my M.D." He shook hands solemnly with his new friend.

Back to Sewanee, Tennessee and the University of the South, Oscar worked with new zeal. His goal was now very near. It would not be easy, the life of a pioneer, but here, a country doctor was needed desperately. His closest friend, Everett Lain had gone to Vanderbilt for this term where larger clinics were available in his chosen specialty, but Oscar was too busy to feel lonely.

Just before the Christmas holidays, on December 15, 1899, Oscar was called into the office of the Dean, J. S. Cain, M.D. He went with some apprehension, as the examinations were completed the week before. He had felt that his grades would be at least passing, but suppose he was wrong!

Dr. Cain rose when he entered the room and extended his hand. "Congratulations, Doctor," he smiled. "I have here an official paper which says that your examinations were satisfactory. This means that on the day of commencement, you will receive the degree of Medical Doctor. In my thinking, your title is Doctor already."

"Thank you, sir," Dr. Newman said humbly. "This is the happiest day of my life."

"There will be happier," the dean assured him. "But there will be sadness and discouragement, too.

However, it is my opinion you have the courage and dedicated purpose to overcome whatever difficulty you may have to face."

Nearly a half century later, on April 26, 1948, Dr. Newman received a letter from Arthur Chitty, alumni secretary of his alma mater nominating him for "Sewanee's outstanding living medical alumnus." His was to be a much greater life than he could imagine at the time he received his degree.

In the spring, Doctor set out for his destination by way of Ohio, where he visited his family. He had his diploma, his doctor's certificate and a precious few surgical instruments. At this point, he had acquired one other possession, a cadaver which would become the skeleton virtually all medical doctors had in those days.

He was welcomed home joyfully, but the folks were not overjoyed to have the cadaver. "I'd like to process it first thing," Doctor told them. "Most of the flesh has been removed, but the remainder will have to be boiled off in water. It won't be a pretty job, but of course, I'll do it alone."

Though in perfect accord with Doctor's projects for advancement, the family denied him the privilege of boiling the cadaver either in the house or in the yard. So, young Newman, now twenty-four years old, hauled a vat and the cadaver into a secluded spot in the hills where he proceeded to finish the job he had to do.

CHAPTER III

EARLY DAYS AT OLD GRAND

Doctor stepped off the train at Higgins, Texas and went into the small station alongside the tracks, a handsome young man with a surgical kit that just fit in his hip pocket and exactly $2.50 in his wallet. At the door stood a strapping pioneer, leaning against the jamb and chewing thoughtfully. "Howdy, stranger," he said jovially.

"Good morning," Doctor said. "How does one get to Grand, Oklahoma Territory from here?"

"Well, now I'd say this is your lucky day. I'm just about to start to Grand with the mail and I'd be right glad for your company. Name's Anzley Ellis."

"Newman," said the other.

"Why, of course now. You're the doctor we've been hoping would settle with us."

Doctor climbed aboard the mail hack and they started the journey. The time was May, 1900 and the prairie was teeming with new life. The cottonwoods rustled gently in the wind as it whipped unabated across the Cheyenne-Arapaho country. Here and there, young children gazed at the strangers passing their dugouts and sod shanties. Homes of any kind were few and far between; at this time there was not a house between Grand and

Early days at old Grand, showing some of Doctor's closest friends in 1901. Left to right, Dr. O. C. Newman, R. E. Johnson (his own cousin), A. S. (Sid) Burran and J. C. Wright.

Gage, and no fences. Law and order were kept with difficulty at times and cattle rustling was fairly easy without fences. A couple of years before Doctor's arrival at Grand, one hundred fifty branded cattle hides were found in a well.

As the South Canadian spread before them, Doctor was a bit apprehensive about the hack, but Ellis prodded the horses to plunge in. "This is the shallowest point," he said.

"I'll try to remember that," Doctor declared, making a mental note of the clump of willows and other surroundings. The village of Grand lay just ahead and as they pulled into town, a number of citizens gathered around, shaking hands with the new doctor.

He stood a bit awkwardly as they began drifting away, then Anzley Ellis asked, "Where are you staying, Doc?"

"I'm afraid I don't know. Could you suggest any place?"

"Mother Walck's, I'd say. Come along, I'll go with you."

A kindly old couple, Mr. and Mrs. Adam Walck, made him welcome at the frame hotel right away though he explained that the $2.50 was all he could pay now, with more depending on earnings from the practice he hoped to establish.

In a few days, Doctor had met everyone in Grand, which was the county seat of Day county. Population of the county was some 350 souls. Seven years later, with statehood, old Day county was split up, much of it forming what is now Ellis county, Oklahoma.

He always approached the untamed cow pony cautiously, and Frog (so named for his wild leaps) invariably entertained with a round of pitching.

One generous man offered to loan to the new doctor a sprightly bronco by the name of Frog for making calls. Though tremendously appreciated, he always approached the untamed cow pony cautiously, and Frog (so named for his wild leaps) invariably entertained with a round of pitching. Being a tenderfoot, Doctor required that some seasoned cowpuncher first mount until the pitching quieted. A little later, he bought the horse and a saddle, with promise to pay as soon as possible. But his gain for nearly two years was practically nothing "not on account of my extravagant living, but the honest people I attended were financially stranded."

The man who sold the saddle was soon dunning him weekly. The time came when the man's wife was soon to be confined and Doctor saw a way to square the debt. Unfortunately, however, when the baby was born, a midwife was called in. But the end was not yet. Following childbirth, infection set in, and three calls later Doctor had paid the seven dollar saddle debt.

Meantime, Doctor was living in embarrassment at Mother Walck's, who carried him along with only a dollar once in a while. It was necessary to pick up side jobs, and being a willing and capable worker, he was soon not only the physician but served also as deputy county clerk, deputy county treasurer, worked in the judge's office, helped to run the postoffice which was in one corner of a storeroom and worked in the town saloon. He carried keys to every office in the courthouse.

The time came when Doctor's three dollar poll tax had to be paid, and like the more down-and-out men of Grand, he picked up a shovel and worked on the road for three days.

In the fall of 1901, parties shipping cattle brought small pox on Eller Flat and Hackberry, west of the Antelope Hills. It was not long until the disease had swept the country. The county allowed Doctor a dollar for each vaccination and at the close of the epidemic, he was paid more than five hundred dollars.

With great satisfaction, he paid the landlady $152, the full amount of his indebtedness to her, and paid his board a month in advance. Frank Burnet, the county treasurer had stood good for Doctor's drug bill and from the first purchase of medicine for $11.35 until he was able to pay, the amount had become considerable. With great pleasure, he proceeded by horseback to Higgins, Texas and paid in full his drug account of $53.00. Doctor would ride all day seeing patients then work until midnight on the county books. Most calls for a doctor came when he was "busy mixing drinks, posting the treasurer's ledger, or emptying the mail sack." When somebody wanted his mail, or was seeking a marriage license, he would have to hunt up Doctor, anywhere in town.

One day while mixing drinks, a powerful chap, a little the worse for drink demanded that Doctor drink with him. "I never touch the dirty stuff," the young man said. "Thank you, anyway."

"Oh, a sissy, huh? Well, I say have a drink."

The saloon keeper stepped up to the tough. "No, not a sissy, just a better man than most. See that you don't pester this young feller anymore." It was the last time Doctor had trouble of that nature.

But there was imminent danger of another kind in the fifty-mile horseback trip Doctor made frequently to Higgins, Texas. No one ever suspected that he carried money in his saddle bags from the county treasurer's office to deposit in the bank.

46 . . .

To the townspeople, he was merely making another professional call.

There were no bridges and Doctor made calls for many miles around in the Territory and Texas, over practically impassable roads and across swollen streams. When the Canadian was at floodtide, there was great danger in crossing.

One spring morning, a man came riding into town, out of breath, he and his horse covered with mud. "Please hurry, Doctor," he panted. "It's the Spence young 'uns. Third one took bad today. 'Low them children all got diphtheria."

The Spence place was fifteen miles south, across the river in Roger Mills. Doctor saddled his horse and started across the river, avoiding a known strip of quicksand. The angry, raging mass of muddy water swirled around the horse's body and suddenly, the footing was gone. The animal floundered, then rallied bravely at Doctor's kindly but insistent urging. Once they reached the bank, they had been swept downstream more a mile.

The children were in serious condition and it was a hard fight throughout the day and all night to keep them alive. The young father went down to the river the next morning and found it had risen ten additional feet.

"Doctor, it would be too dangerous for you to attempt the crossing," he said. "But if you must, then I'll go across with you."

"These children can't do without me yet," the young doctor said gravely. He stayed three days, scarcely sleeping until they were better. On that last afternoon, Spence was gone from home for a while, bringing back thirty dollars which he had received for a young beef to pay Doctor.

"This is all I have right now," the father said.

Doctor handed it back. "You'll likely need this. Maybe you can see me some other time."

Doctor inspired honesty and loyalty in those who knew him. A rancher from quite some distance is a case in point. The man had suffered from chills and fever and Doctor had given him a round of bitter quinine in the new-fangled gelatine capsules. Several days later, the rancher, obviously much better, rode into Grand in search of Dr. Newman.

"Here you are, Doctor," he said handing him a small box. "I took it all like you said, and I've brought back your little bottles." Inside the box were all the empty capsules.

Times were hard for all in those days. Doctor often observed the easy going contentment of the Indians when they came through the country as the seasons changed. They camped on Pony creek, hunting and fishing. In the fall, they returned to pick persimmons and always looked well fed. The settlers were not always faring so well.

One evening about sundown after a twelve-mile ride to see a woman patient, the son told Doctor that she was feeling better and they would have supper first thing. They sat down to the table on which was only a dishpan full of clabbered milk. Without apology, it was sliced off to serve for supper and Doctor was asked if he preferred salt or sugar on his clabber.

On another occasion, he was far out in the country when dinner time came, so he stopped

48 . . .

at the first dwelling he came upon. It was customary for any traveler, even a stranger to stop any place for a free meal.

The rancher welcomed him into his humble home. They discussed the weather for a little, then the lady of the house came from the lean-to kitchen. Taking the cloth off the churn which stood warming by the fireplace, she wiped the baby's chin with it, then said, "Sit up and have dinner."

On the table were sour dough biscuits and a can of molasses. Doctor wondered in vain when they would bring on the rest of the meal. But that was all.

"Too bad about our neighbors down the road a-ways," said the host. "I hear tell they had a lot of hard luck and his family is living on ground corn. I'll go down today and take them something to eat."

Doctor was unable to spend anything on clothes for his first two years in Grand, and if anyone

Frog often waited while Doctor had skimpy meals with the settlers, sometimes nothing more than clabbered milk, or sourdough biscuits and molasses.

wondered how he managed, a certain hunter could have told. The hunter had accidentally shot off the end of his finger and entered the six-by-twelve foot office Doctor had acquired along the end of a store building.

No one was to be seen, so the patient parted the curtain to Doctor's "living quarters" and there he sat in his underwear, mending his wornout and only pair of trousers. At the time, several hundreds of dollars were owed to him, even at the low fees, by people who could never pay. At this time, Doctor was sleeping on the floor of his office in warm weather and on a counter in the adjoining store in winter.

Occasionally, some man objected to Doctor's fees, even when never paid. One bright, summer day, Doctor relaxed an hour at a community picnic in a shady grove at Grand. Contentedly sipping lemonade, he felt at peace with the world when a rough character began loudly to complain and verbally abuse him.

"Imagines he's better than most, I reckon, charging any price he pleases to suffering people." And then he took a swing.

Doctor looked around into the angry face of a rancher he readily recognized. The week before, Doctor had charged fifty cents for riding out and pulling an abscessed tooth for the man's wife. Usually of mild, even temper, Doctor suddenly saw red. Dashing for the heckler, he planned to beat him to a pulp, but friends restrained him and the rancher left there fast.

Some outlaw brothers, famous and infamous in pioneer Oklahoma history were close acquaintances, and Doctor saw good points in their characters which he hoped considerate friendship would bring out. One day, he was attending the wife of a settler who was a sister to these outlaws. He spent the night and next morning after breakfast, he stepped outside for a smoke.

On returning to the room, the outlaw brothers were there, cursing the husband while the woman cried helplessly. One of the fellows dropped his hand to his gun and declared: "I'm a good notion to shoot him."

Doctor grabbed the outlaw's hand. "Get out of here if you can't act like a gentleman in a sickroom. I know your sister has a kind husband; it's you fellows causing the tears, and if you know what's good for you, you'd better hit the grit." The outlaw brothers got!

Doctor decided after he was free of indebtness that he was entitled to invest in some personal satisfaction. He had always wanted to become a Mason, since his father had belonged to that fraternity. So, in 1902, he rode horseback seventy miles on a trip to Texmo, Oklahoma Territory and was accepted in that Lodge No. 56.

Quin Walck was a close friend to Doctor in those early days at Grand. The two young men slept together in a garret room and Quin recalled many years later that his sleep was never unbroken as calls came at all hours regardless of the weather. Sometimes, Doctor didn't get to bed at all.

One evening, Quin was abed and Doctor had just stumbled home exhausted and was sitting on the bed trying to get undressed. A pounding came on the door and a distraught man pushed it open. "Hurry, Doc, hurry! It's my wife. She took bad quick. Maternity case."

Doctor mumbled and tried to rise. "Can you make it?" Quin said, getting up to help him.

"I guess I'd better go," Doctor sighed. The journey was more than twenty miles and a driving snowstorm had brought paralyzing cold. Doctor did not return until afternoon of the next day.

During the preceding summer, a large, mournful owl had the habit of perching on the highest tree in the Walck yard and serenading the gentry with doleful sounds all through the night. After a particularly tiresome trip, Doctor said to his friend one moon-flooded midnight: "Quin, I wish you would get your gun and see if you can't eliminate that old hooter."

The young fellow loaded up and blasted the nuisance from the tree and no more was heard. After breakfast, the two went in search of the dead creature and found it very much alive and with only a wing broken. Doctor began to laugh.

"Hey, what's so funny?" Quin wanted to know.

"I must be a genius; I just thought of the best way to dispose of this pest. Let's carry him over and put him in bed with that drunk in the side room of the saloon."

Each took hold of a wing and though they succeeded in their mission, yet while walking, the owl got hold of Doctor by the seat and caused itself to be remembered for a long time.

As time went on, Grand was a thriving little

town. Hi Walck was always known as the founder and the first clerk of Day county. O. E. Null began the filing of abstracts in longhand and later owned the first typewriter in those parts. The **Day County Progress** was the first newspaper, established by Cap Mitchell. Two others followed. First lawyers included S. A. Miller, C. B. Leedy and Ben F. Barnett. E. G. Rader and Sam Cupp had the general stores, while George Rader was the earliest sheriff. Charles Swindall, just out of law school was county attorney.

The settlers believed in education and somehow had a school house in every district, built of sod or green, rawhide cottonwood lumber. They had crude seats, a wood stove in which cow chips were used for fuel and strict teachers who instilled the fundamentals of high ideals, self reliance, honor and integrity. Some of the earliest teachers were Anna Moorehead, Myrtle Bowles and Bell Carper. The school house was also used for church services, pie socials and literaries. The settlers were active in participation entertainment; ball games, horse races and dancing.

Day county was so named for a man by that name who paid $100 for the honor of building the first courthouse. This was a part of the Cheyenne-Arapaho lands arranged by treaty signed at Medicine Lodge on October 28, 1867. The Indian tribes accepted their lands in severalty in 1890, and in 1893, the Cherokee outlet was thrown open for homesteading on 160-acre tracts, with the settler required to establish residence and cultivate the land.

The man with the hoe arrived about the same time as the cattleman. The latter would locate on a stream, place his land filing so he could control the water, then stake off enough land for his needs. These first settlers were sure the farmers could not stay it out and the plains would remain for the cattlemen. When Doctor arrived, some of the cattlemen were Frank and George Walton, Frank Nickerson, M. F. Word, John Griffis, O. H. Richards, George Carr, John McQuigg, Charles and Hayden Killgore and Ira Eddleman.

Fortunately there was no animosity between the two factions. As homesteaders came pouring in, the cow men leased them land in their own pastures. It looked like easy money, for surely the tenderfoot, without dwelling facilities, would be unable to "prove up" his claim. But the settlers were mostly of pioneer stock and they stayed. The cattlemen saw their pasture lands taken. The homesteaders began farming and the Herd Law became necessary to protect their crops. Still, there was no open conflict. Personal difficulties were settled honorably and petty thievery among the citizens was unknown.

To prove that this was an agricultural country, the farmers put on a county fair in the fall of 1901. Among the prize exhibits was a watermelon weighing one hundred pounds which inspired the Santa Fe railway to sponsor an advertising campaign of the agricultural resources in its territory. The watermelon was lovingly hauled about to show at several other fairs and always took the blue ribbon.

The first fraternal organization in Grand was the Woodmen of the World. Other lodges instituted soon after were the Odd Fellows and Masons of which first officers were William Suthers, Otis Richards, David Hogg, O. C. Newman (who moved

54 . . .

his affiliation from Texmo to Grand), Joseph Smith, G. A. Bigelow, O. E. Null, A. A. Bennett and George Rader.

Law and medicine had come to Grand at about the same time. That fall, after Doctor had arrived in May, there were three murder cases on the court docket. There was a grand jury, a petit jury and the whole legal works.

By 1902, Doctor had obtained a buggy and carried in the back his medical library and supplies. He also acquired a trained nurse, Mrs. Dora McIntosh who, with her husband and son, Harold, had come from Kansas and proved up on a claim. Nurse McIntosh was fearless, sturdy and softly sympathetic. Doctor carried his operating table strapped to the side of his buggy, and surgery was performed in the patient's homes, using chloroform as an anesthetic.

Before the nurse came along, various men consented to go along with Doctor to administer the anesthetic in perhaps bungling, but big-hearted manner. One of these Good Samaritans was Belford Habekott. Surgery was, in the minds of the patients, a final resort, but many an appendix was separated from Day Countains who lived long, healthy lives afterward.

CHAPTER IV

THE PEOPLE NEED HIM

They were his people, these pioneers who straggled into the Panhandle country just after the turn of the century. Doctor loved them all, the bewhiskered, tobacco-chewing homesteaders with faded, patched overalls; the barefoot, tow-headed youngsters with freckled and sun-baked faces; the brave, clear-eyed women going uncomplainingly about their hard tasks and harder childbearing.

By buckboard and covered wagon, they streamed onto the virgin prairie from the north and the east, determined to face and overcome the hardships of a raw, frontier life. They came with their farm animals, a pair of tough mules pulling the wagon, a squealing hog or so crated at the end-gate, a dry cow tied to the back. Usually, a couple of bony hounds trotted a little ahead of the assembly.

Bravely they staked their claims near the spot where the mighty Canadian encircled the Antelope Hills; where the sand dunes shifted beneath the relentless winds; where the black diamond rattler slithered through the purple sage, bunch grass and bluestem; where black, choking dust storms and raging prairie fires vied for fearfulness with the stunning blizzards, the vicious tornadoes and the devastating floods on the Canadian. By night, they listened to the blood-curdling howls of the lobo wolf and the incessant yapping of the coyote. Bobcats roamed about, making dangerous any venture into the darkness.

But the living was not all bad. When spring skipped on little-lamb feet across the plains, the cottonwood leaf buds responded to the kiss of the soft breezes and spread a pale green canopy over the warm earth. The hearts of the people were filled with hope in the spring, for it meant a new beginning, a fresh opportunity to make a good crop with which to ease the hardships of the next winter. Spirits were high by the time the yucca bloomed. The territorial streams were full of fish, and wild game was abundant. From these sources many were kept alive who would otherwise have gone hungry; or worse, would have been forced to give up their claims and leave.

Trapping was a fine way of increasing the merger income in the winter. Ordinary skunk hides brought seven or eight cents each; a pure black one was worth the bonus sum of fifty cents. A man could eat a cottontail rabbit and sell his hide for one cent, not bad when you realize that three cents would buy a pound of dry beans.

Something about the open country made large appetites. A good standby was the lowly corndodger which was baked in an old-fashioned oven over coals of the open fire. Coffee was coarsely ground by hand and made into a brew so strong that it would "float an iron wedge."

The winter of 1903 brought a record blizzard over the Panhandle country, with snow and ice twenty-six inches deep. Illness was at a record high and Doctor made his way doggedly through drifts, facing into the teeth of the storm to bring relief to the suffering. Not all patients could be saved, however, for no amount of medicine or attention could overcome the raw exposure endured by most of the people.

All too many lived in dugouts and sod houses. Those houses which were built of cottonwood had been hastily thrown together while the lumber was green; then when it seasoned, wide cracks appeared in the walls.

Solon Porter, a settler in Grand told of that terrible winter in his own cottonwood shack, where he lived alone. His bed was a box, four by six feet and he had a couple of blankets which put him among the lucky. He spent the days and nights in bed, crawling out only to fry some fat meat and make batter cakes. He had picked up a box of cow chips before the snowstorm and learned how to cook a meal with a minimum of this fuel.

Illness was at a record high and Doctor made his way doggedly through drifts, facing into the teeth of the storm to bring relief to the suffering.

After several days of this, a neighbor man came to his door to borrow flour for a large family of starving children. The neighbor had wrapped his feet in rolls of gunny sacks in an effort to prevent frostbite. No person ever turned away another in need, but shared equally and gladly. It was a sort of unspoken code of the frontier.

Pneumonia was an enemy to be particularly dreaded when blizzards descended upon the plains. Too often, the monster had progressed too far before the family of the patient sent for the doctor.

One bitterly cold night, Doctor asked his friend, Quin Walck to go along in the buggy on a call across the river. They set out through inky blackness, shivering against the howling teeth of the storm. Crossing at a shallow point where the ice was thick enough to support buggy, team and men, they came safely to the opposite side. Quin heard Doctor sigh with relief when they reached the hard-frozen land, for he was not always so lucky as to avoid a break-through.

Muffling their faces with gloved hands, they rode in silence until the faithful horses, by some instinct, went the way almost without guidance. The place was a dilapidated part-dugout with a ragged quilt hung up for a door.

Inside were a woman, man and three children. The two older youngsters, the patients, were curled up in a "nest" which could hardly be called a bed. As Doctor examined them, they whined more in fear than in suffering. The mother, too, whined, begging him not to hurt her children. They had pneumonia, as Doctor had feared.

During the examination, he glanced from time to time at the baby, apparently some eighteen months old, sitting on the dirt floor. After ministering to the others, he turned to the little one. With a cry of alarm, the woman swooped the child up in her arms. "Don't!" she cried. "Let the baby be—do you hear?"

"Surely you don't mind if I examine him?" Doctor asked quietly. "I don't like the color in his cheeks."

"Never you mind," the woman declared. "There's nothing wrong with him."

"Please, madam," said Doctor. "I'm afraid the little one is worse off than the others. My conscience wouldn't let me sleep if I didn't make every effort to help him."

But his reasoning and pleading were in vain. Before he could get back to see the other children a few days later, the baby had died. After several more trips to minister to the older ones, they recovered.

Many were the times when someone would come across Doctor napping in his buggy at the side of the road, taking advantage of a few spare minutes to rest his body and mind before he was again called out.

Doctor enjoyed passing along the things that struck him as funny. One time, he visited a man in Grand, who groaned loudly while his wife related at great length the many ailments he suffered. She counted them one by one on her fingers, and running out of fingers, she finally declared: "Well, I'll tell you, Doc, his whole carcass is out of clatter."

In earlier days, when Doctor was still riding a borrowed bronc, his guide was a river sleuth named George Wilcox. Wilcox taught Doctor, and the horse, some tricks to outsmart the surging Canadian. Rapid goosestepping would usually get the horse across a bar of quicksand and the animal learned the art right away. Doctor would hold his bag of instruments and medicine high above his head to avoid having it swept away. On only one occasion was the physician divested of everything, including his hat.

This time, the call was a typhoid fever case from John McQuigg down the river seven miles on the opposite side, by the Antelope Hills. George Howlett went along as he frequently did, being a close friend. George was riding a horse named Brown Jug while Doctor was mounted on Frog. The river was at flood stage with "bottomless" holes and cross currents. Doctor got excited and rode off in a deep place, and to keep from getting his feet wet, he lifted them and hooked them in old Frog's flanks. Whereupon, Frog started pitching and bucked him off in the middle of the river. His pill bag having gone with everything else that could be lost, Doctor had to return to Grand for dry, borrowed clothes and more medicine.

Oscar and George hunted a great deal before Doctor's practice became so time-consuming. Both being poor boys, they shared the expenses for shotgun shells, twenty-five for twenty-five cents. One would put in a dime and the other fifteen cents, then reverse the contributions next time, as neither could afford a quarter outlay at once. Often, they would not shoot to kill; only to cripple small game, then Doctor would proceed to do experimental operations.

George and Oscar went frequently to square

dances, and though he later became adept at the art, Doctor learned the hard way. Jake Bull gave a "big one" at his ranch, attended by Joseph (Dock) Smith, Bert Wagner, Obe Hail, Anzley Ellis, Bill Suthers, Quin Walck, Chet Null, Emmett Alcorn, George Howlett, Doctor Newman, Ed Carpenter, Tobe Wheat, Milton Crawford, Fred Timms, Sid Burran, John Richards, John and Billy McGuinty, John Griffis, "Six-Shooter Andy," Bob Johnson, a cousin, and their lady escorts.

Millard Word was doing the fiddling. They got Doctor into "Cage the Bird" and "Close the Door." Two turns and he was lost, so the rest of the dancers in the set shoved him around where he was supposed to move. Finally, Doctor threw up his hands and shouted, "Somebody catch me, I don't know where I'm going."

They all stopped dancing and began to laugh. It was then that somebody announced that a prize was hidden in the top of the tallest tree by the house; it would go to anyone who could retrieve it.

"That's for me," Doctor declared. "I learned to shinny up trees where they grow tall in Ohio."

He was almost to the top when a limb broke beneath his weight, and down Doctor crashed into a pile of brush. He was scratched up some, but worse, his trousers were torn off. Sid Burran went indoors and got a pair of Jake Bull's britches, made to fit a man six feet, two. Doctor had to roll up the cuffs several times, but returned to the party something of a hero. He learned a lot about square dancing that night.

For a man with only one pair to his name, Doctor had an extraordinary amount of bad luck with his britches. About nine one morning, a couple of fellows from over on Sand Creek rode into town and stopped in front of the blacksmith shop. All the loafers moseyed over to get into whatever argument might ensue. The Sand Creek boys were in a jovial mood.

"Looks like you fellows would be out getting some game," one of them remarked. "There are lots of quirlies (squirrels) out on the flat."

Lee Collins, returned from the Spanish and American war, and garbed now in his uniform, said: "Come to think of it, I'm pretty fed up on rabbits. What do you say, Doc—want to go out there hunting with me?"

"That's quite a long walk," Doctor said.

Anzley Ellis spoke up. "I expect you could borrow Papa's little mules and hack."

The elder Ellis was generous. "Sure, boys, but you'll have to hold the mules when you shoot. They're downright skittish when it comes to guns."

"How about the girls going along to hold them when we get out to hunt?" Doctor suggested, indicating two of Anzley's sisters.

All agreed to the arrangement and proceeded to the flat. In something over an hour, the loafers heard a team coming from the east at a hard pace. Around a bend came the little mules in a run, Lee Collins standing up and slapping their rumps with the lines to induce more speed, while Doctor and the girls hung on for dear life.

They clattered to a stop in front of the saloon, and Doctor, hat in one hand and gun in the other jumped from the hack without a word and headed in a run for the Walck hotel.

"What ails **him**?" Anzley asked, scratching his head in bewilderment.

"Well, it's funny, but not so funny at that," Collins explained. "Doctor bought a pint of turpentine in Higgins yesterday, put it in his hip pocket and forgot to take it out. Reckon the stopper came out and wet the seat of Doc's pants. It mighty nigh set Doc on fire."

The next morning, Anzley and a few others were loafing at Frank Burnet's store when they heard horses running. All went to the door and saw a rig coming, down in the draw just north of town.

"It's Bill," the storekeeper said. "He's after Doc. They're expecting a new youngster at his place." The excited man drew up to the group and asked for Doctor. "Ain't been down all morning," Burnet said. "Ask for him up at the hotel."

The rig was off at a swift gait. The expectant father pounded on the front door. No answer. He could hear Mother Walck in the kitchen, so he went around to the back. "Howdy, Bill," the kindly old lady greeted him. "How's your folks?"

"Not so good. My wife's down sick. Where's Doc?" His voice trembled and his hands shook like an aspen in the wind.

"Now just you calm yourself, my boy. This is not the first baby ever born. Doctor's upstairs in bed. Went a-huntin' yesterday. Spilled his medicine and spoiled his britches. I've not had time yet to wash 'em. But I'll get a pair of Grandpa's for him to wear. He'll be right down." Two minutes later,

Doctor, pill satchel and baggy trousers were in the rig, headed out across the draw. It was one of his first confinement cases.

Late the following afternoon, just as the sun was setting, they saw him coming. He alighted from Bill's hack and the man turned around and headed away. "Well, Doc," someone remarked. "How'd you make out?"

"All right," Doctor said wearily. "There'll be another Democrat in twenty-one years."

Doctor was beginning to be interested in politics about that time. The homesteaders and cattlemen were at cross purposes, what with crops growing and cattle roaming the range. Doctor ran for county treasurer on the Free Grass ticket, along with A. S. (Sid) Burran for county clerk. People in the eastern part of the county were mostly supporters of the Herd Law ticket, as the two friends found when they went "electioneering" in that settlement. They decided to go into the other side of the county where they would find more encouragement.

Reaching Grand late at night, they were exhausted and their riding horses' heads drooped. The little courthouse was all lighted up. They rode by and looked in a window. There, sprawled out on a desk was a man, very dead.

"It's Burnham!" Sid cried. "Politics must be warming up over in our part of the county. That man was your opponent, you know."

Doctor drew a long, ragged breath. "I appreciate loyalty, but this was carrying it much too far. Anyway, Burnham can't vote against me now."

The farmers were confident during that campaign. Things were looking up for them. Quite a number of copies of the **Kansas City Star** piled into the Grand postoffice each week; the homesteaders could subscribe for twenty-five cents a year, and they studied religiously the articles in it, expecting to improve their farming methods.

But regardless of which side they were on, homesteader and Herd Law ticket or cattleman and Free Grass ticket, every man, woman and child in Day county respected and needed the dedicated and courageous young doctor. He had completely won their confidence.

CHAPTER V

A HELPMEET FOR DOCTOR

Pearl Smith stirred restlessly in her sleep, feeling subconsciously that something was wrong. From the depth of slumber, she could hear the coyotes barking over on the creek, and the regular breathing of her husband, Dock. She tried to stir herself awake but she was so terribly tired, what with the baby almost due, and little Lyman had been so fretful all day.

Lyman! She was instantly awake, sitting upright in bed and fumbling for the little son lying between them. The child was burning with fever and his breath came in harsh gasps. Pearl shook her husband awake.

"You'll have to get Dr. Newman," the girl sobbed.

"Is the baby coming?" he cried, propping up on an elbow.

"No, it's Lyman. He's in a bad way. Hurry!"

Dock threw the saddle on a horse and headed in a run for Mother Walck's hotel. The time was April, 1901 and the night was soft and pleasant. How could the little fellow have taken such a cold in this nice, spring weather, after keeping well through the winter, with hardly more than sniffles? That afternoon, he had brought in a horse thief from far across country, in line with his duty as sheriff of Day county. Gentle Joseph (Dock) Smith had wondered then how it would feel to be locked up, when outside it was sweet, breathless April.

Fortunately, Doctor was not out on call and they raced back to the Smith home. The girl-mother was crying helplessly over the sick youngster and when they appeared, she cried, "Thank God! Please help him, Doctor."

It was a hard fight with pneumonia and Doctor stayed beside the child. Some time the following day, Dock asked a kind neighbor to send a buggy after his sister, a young girl of seventeen, who lived at Ural, near Chickasha. Miss Della Smith, a lovely, Texas-born girl arrived soon at the home of her brother to help with the cooking and caring for the sick.

Doctor came and went, doing what he could, noticing nothing but the little patient. And then, one morning, he straightened up wearily and glanced outside. Della sat there in the warm sunshine with a bit of needlework in her hands.

Doctor turned to Dock. "Unless my eyes fail me, there is the prettiest young lady I've ever seen. Who is she?"

The sheriff looked at Della. It was true, his little sister had grown up. Her skin was like ivory, tinted with rose, and her large brown eyes complemented the mass of her shining dark hair.

"Why, she is pretty at that," Dock marvelled. "Come out and I'll make you acquainted."

Doctor took the small hand of the beautiful creature, who lowered her head and blushed becomingly.

70 . . .

Strange, the warm feeling he had, as if suddenly, everything took on a deeper meaning.

The crisis in little Lyman's illness approached, and never had the condition of a patient been of such vital, personal concern to the young physician. The child was not going to pull through. Doctor suffered agony of spirit seeing the little boy's life slipping away. He had always known that some of his patients would have to die, but now that the first loss was apparent, the young doctor felt bewildered and defeated.

After the inevitable had occurred, the friendship between young Newman and Della Smith grew and deepened. Their courtship lasted through the summer when hot dust whipped across the land, through the mud and cold of fall and winter. When April came again, the two were thinking of marriage.

Doctor was still financially behind. Though his practice had increased steadily, the people could not pay. Many were the times when he could not see his betrothed except in brief stops when returning from a call, and before starting out again. Della was young, but from the beginning, she understood how it would be, being married to Doctor who belonged first of all to the suffering folk of Day county.

The young man was walking one noon toward the Walck boarding house thinking of Della and wishing for a financial turn for the better. He could not possibly marry her yet, though she subconsciously filled his thoughts while he went about visiting the small pox patients and attending to multiple duties at the courthouse at night.

There was something about the convenience of the stile, in this new country of hardships that somehow reminded Doctor of home in the staid Ohio valley. He smiled as he approached the stile.

First of all was that large board bill. The worry about it nagged him day and night. He could send home to Ohio and the folks would gladly help, but Oscar was determined to make his own way, somehow. Maybe soon—

It was late May again and the green of nature spread everywhere. Doctor took a deep breath of the clean air. All about him was a grove of trees and just ahead, the stile, steps built up and over the barbed wire fence. There was something about the convenience of the stile, in this new country of hardships, that somehow reminded Doctor of home in the staid Ohio valley. Without consciously doing so, he smiled as he approached the stile.

Descending the other side, he met his host, elderly Adam Walck and the old man's grandson, Chester Null. "Any new cases of the small pox?" the youngster asked eagerly. It was plain from the look on Chester's face that he idolized Doctor.

"I'm afraid so," Doctor said, tousling his young friend's hair with an affectionate hand. Then he turned to the older man. "Mr. Walck," he said. "I was on my way to dinner, but I'm just so far behind with my board bill that I'm ashamed to eat. There are simply not enough people here, able to pay, to justify my staying to practice and I'm thinking of another location. I've had a chance to take over the practice of a retiring physician in a town in Arkansas, and—"

"Hold on, young feller," Mr. Walck said. "Listen to me. That board bill is bothering you much more than us. I wonder if you realize that the satisfaction of having you here is worth more to us than what you owe, even if we all stay well."

Doctor thought about it a moment. Mr. Walck had six sons and two daughters in this vicinity, all with families. Yes, he was needed here, and it was a moment of weakness to consider leaving Grand. Doctor was heartily ashamed of himself. He shook Adam Walck's hand. "I hope Mother Walck has a big dinner. I'm hungry!"

Always afterward, the memory of this incident returned to Doctor when he approached the turnstile. It was not long after this time until the county was able to pay Doctor $555 for his services during the small pox epidemic. In addition to his many other duties, he was paid a little for being county superintendent of public health, a newly created office in the new settlement.

Following payment of his debts, Doctor bought a new suit and went to the sheriff's home to claim his girl. "It won't be easy, Della, this life we'll share together; at least not for a long, long time, but I need you."

The shy young girl put her hand in his and Doctor held on tightly. For him, it was the beginning, all over again.

On a late summer day, Doctor sat down and penned a very important letter.

County Superintendent of
Public Health of Day County
Grand, Oklahoma, August 27th, 1902

Mrs. Smith
Chickasha, Indian Territory

My dear Friend:
Necessarily denying myself the pleasure of personally seeing you, that I may ask of **you** more

than I can ever hope to repay, without elaborate explanatory remarks of my former morality, I am free to inform you my past life is subject to investigation and my informal request shall be definite and explicit. No doubt you have been informed, previous to now, by your **daughter**, Miss Della of our marriage in the near future and with due courtesy and respect toward you, I ask **your** consent..

Hoping it will ever be harmonious and agreeable, I shall **ever** bear in mind silence gives **consent.** Expecting the same courtesy, I wait an early reply.

Yours very truly,
O. C. Newman

Word began circulating around town right away that a public wedding of great importance would occur in the Woodmen of the World Hall on September 18th. Identity of the contracting parties was kept secret as long as possible, but from the post-office at the south end of Main street to the Walck hotel up on the hill at the northern extremity, people were making good guesses.

The women got out their tubs and rubboards and "did up" the best "bib and tucker" for every member of the family. A big social event meant feasting, and in typical pioneer manner, everyone furnished food, so the kindly wives of all the county began to save and plan ahead. There was also the matter of bringing to the wedding a gift for the couple, and all really close friends did so.

The Certificate of Holy Matrimony, still in good condition today, was issued at Grand, Oklahoma on September 18, 1902, with the information that Oscar Clarence Newman was twenty-five, born in Ohio

to Mesheck Herdman Newman and Sarah Johnson
Newman, that Della Smith was eighteen, born in
Texas to L. P. Smith and Matilda Tatum Smith.
The certificate further stated that witnesses were
S. Y. Cupp, F. W. Allen and A. S. Burran, and was
officiated by F. M. Sandford, J. P. and Rev. David
Hogg.

Doctor particularly chose September 18 as his
wedding date, Della always in agreement with his
wishes, because it was the birth date of his honored
father. Later, another great occurrence in his life
would come on that same date.

In the preceding weeks, talk was on hardly any
subject other than the big wedding to be. Alex
Hutchison was perhaps the least suspected bachelor
in Grand, but he offered all manner of odds in wag-
ers that he would be the lucky groom but, as one
oldtimer put it, "Alex always managed to have a
string to all of his bills, so he could call them
back." Tight-fisted he might have been, but the
old bachelor opened up his purse strings and bought
a number of chickens and turkeys for the good
neighbor women to prepare for the wedding supper.

The **Day County Tribune** described it thus:
"The Woodmen of the World at Grand gave one
of the swellest entertainments on the night of the
18th inst. ever given in Western Oklahoma. The
Doctor is one of Day counties most honored sons
and is especially popular in Masonic and Woodmen
circles, while Miss Della is a most charming, beautiful and popular young lady."

Long before night, virtually all of the 350 residents of Day county had swarmed into Grand, by
buckboard, buggy, hack, horseback, muleback and

76 . . .

on foot. The weather was balmy and warm and the bride did not even wear a light wrap. The Canadian was low and easy to ford, since the fall rains had not yet begun.

Tables were pushed together to form two continuous tables the full length of the hall and specially prepared dishes covered all the space on them. Some people had gone all the distance to Gage, up in the general direction of Woodward to buy some such delicacy as coconut for cakes and pies.

The Woodmen walked in a body to bring the bride and groom to the hall, then, with their red, white and blue axes, they formed an arch under which the couple walked to the front. Mrs. A. A. Bennett at the treasured old foot-pedaled organ provided the traditional wedding march.

David McPherson and Miss Jennie Walck served as best man and maid of honor as they stood before Judge Sandford and Rev. David Hogg. The ceremony was brief and the crowd was utterly silent until Parson Hogg pronounced the benediction. Feasting continued until far into the night.

Some very special guests from outside Grand included "Dr. Fred C. White and sister; Mr. Thomas and sister, of Antelope; Mr. O. G. Galloway, of Streeter; Miss Cora Bigelow, of Higgins, Texas; Miss Libbie Richards, of Rock, Kansas, and Dr. F. W. Allen, of Texmo."

The **Day County Tribune** that week published in full the wedding presents and the donors, as follows: Mr. and Mrs. F. W. Allen, set of initialed silver spoons; Mr. and Mrs. E. E. Shirley, set of silver knives and forks; R. E. Johnson, Japanese tea

Doctor felt rather proud that he was able to get a two-room house right in the heart of Grand, just a stone's throw from the schoolhouse.

set; Miss Hazel Cupp, jelly dish; Miss Ida Null, card receiver; Charles Cupp, sets of cups and saucers; A. S. Burran, molasses pitcher and pepper and salt stand; Mrs. Smith, celery glass; Mr. and Mrs. Sam Cupp, wash bowl and pitcher; Alex Hutchison, set of goblets; Mrs. J. L. Smith, set of dessert dishes and pickle dish.

And Jennie Walck, towel; Hattie Wilson, towel; Cora Bigelow, bread plate; Laura Null, cake plate; Mrs. Bennett, berry dish; Mrs. George Rader, stew pan; Mrs. Mary Walck, quilt; Mrs. Sandford, coffee pot; Mr. and Mrs. O. E. Null, kerosene lamp; Dora S. Johnson, orange spoon and case; Laura Conover, mustache cup and saucer (for him) and decorated cup and saucer (for her); Sarah Hartman, cream pitcher, sugar bowl, lamp mat, chair tidy, silk chair cushion and silk sofa cushion; Mrs. Smith, spoon; Mr. and Mrs. E. H. Wheat, wash tub and wash board; S. A. Miller, sack of flour; Parson Hogg, bedstead; Dean and Dick Miller, broom.

As soon as they could break away, Oscar and Della left the building for the warm, summer night outdoors where a horse and buggy waited. But on the way, they were stopped by a small, freckled-faced lad. He stood awkwardly before the bride holding something wrapped in a back copy of the weekly newspaper.

"I wanted to give you a present," he said, looking down at his wriggling, bare toes. "But I figgered they'd laugh at me if I did, so I didn't put it with the rest. Here," he pushed the parcel into Della's hands. "I raised it myself." Then he took to his heels and ran toward home.

"Hey, now, did I detect tears near the surface when that youngster was talking?" Doctor asked.

Della looked up at him and her own brown eyes swam with happy tears. "Wasn't it touching? That little fellow is only nine years old but he always claimed me for his girl." She tore aside the newspaper and there was the largest sweet potato either of them had ever seen. When they started "keeping house," it lasted for a week and came in handy.

From the wedding celebration, the young doctor and his fair bride were driven to Higgins, Texas through the soft, starry night. Every sound on the prairie seemed gentle and friendly, even the howls of the wolves. Once or twice, Della fell asleep and her head dropped against Oscar's shoulder. If one could have seen Doctor's face at that time, the smile there would have been like a benediction.

Dawn was pink across the eastern sky when they arrived at the little Higgins depot, and soon the train chugged to a stop to take them to Canadian, Texas for a brief honeymoon as guests in the home of his uncle, Dr. A. M. Newman. They could not be gone long, for back at Grand, the people needed their doctor.

The people welcomed them home and helped the young couple to get "straightened out." Doctor felt rather proud that he was able to get a two-room house right in the heart of town, just a stone's throw from the school house, which served also for a church building. Though bare and simple, the house was reasonable protection from the elements and it had a lean-to shed at the back for his rig and horses.

It should be remembered that, until his marriage, Doctor's only method of getting around was by horseback. Della's sheriff brother, Dock, had taken one look at that shed and a sudden inspiration told him what to give his new brother-in-law for a wedding present. A group of townsmen were gathered, talking, in front of the Howlett and Wheat store one day, shortly after the wedding, when Doctor joined them.

"Come along, Doctor," Dock said. "I was just about to go up to the stable and hook up the team and exercise them a little. Like to go along?"

The two drove east from Grand and followed trails for about an hour and a half, then came in just west of the school house. Dock turned out of the road toward Doctor's little house. "Better drop in and see Della a little," he said.

He drove right into the shed at the back and they both climbed down. "Let's unhook them," Dock said, clapping a hand on Doctor's shoulder. "I guess I'll just give you this outfit."

Della set to work with a will to make the new home cheery and livable. Using kerosene and lye

"Come along, Doctor," his new brother-in-law said. "I was just about to exercise the team a little. Like to come along?"

soap, she removed the lettering from flour sacks and with them, created perky little curtains for the windows. She had been taught from early girlhood by her mother, Matilda Smith, that any home, however humble, reflected the personality of the lady of the house. Della had a good collection of scarves and doilies, handmade towels and bed clothing which she had made for her hope chest long before meeting Doctor. Now that they graced her own home, they seemed prettier than ever.

On their first night back from the honeymoon, Doctor was called out to visit a patient, and Della had come to expect that this was to be the pattern of their life together. Frequently, they came pounding at her door while he was out, asking her to have Doctor come quickly just the minute he returned.

That winter, he would come in half frozen, put an extra stick of wood on the fire and sit there warming his chilled fingers and toes for just a few minutes before plunging into the frigid night once more. Watching him from her warm bed, Della's heart overflowed with love and admiration for her young husband. And she made a silent vow, then and there, to spend her life making him as physically comfortable as possible, and lend to him the strength of her faith and confidence in his ability.

Since Doctor had become a family man, he was often paid for professional service with slabs of salt meat, bags of beans and peas, turnips, potatoes, fresh garden products in season, even watermelons and pumpkins. Food prices were very low, and Della could feed her husband and several guests on dry, blackeyed peas boiled with a chunk of fat meat for a cost of only a few pennies. Doctor rarely had time to go hunting or fishing, but being popular with all the people of Grand, Della frequently shared the catch from an afternoon of fishing, or was given a tender young cottontail so that Doctor could feast on a heaping platter of fried rabbit for Sunday dinner.

It was not simple at first for the gently reared girl to skin a rabbit or scrape the scales from a smelly fish. Nor was it easy to bandage a badly bleeding hand or foot while the patient waited for Doctor to return home in the evening. After a few weeks of such experiences, the girl began to be both calm and efficient, and felt happy that she was perhaps becoming a wife worthy of Doctor.

And then, along in the late winter before the ice broke on the Day county creeks, for no reason that she could see, Della became squeamish at the sight of blood. Her appetite, usually voracious out of all proportion to her tiny body, suddenly became squeamish, also. After a while, she told her husband of all her silly symptoms, and he took her lovely face between his big, gentle hands.

"Little Della, it looks as if you are going to present this happy sawbones with an heir."

CHAPTER VI

A TIME OF CHANGE

In the years from 1901 to 1904, Day county became settled, with hardly a quarter section of land vacant. The Newman homestead was listed in the county records as E½ of SW¼ of Sec. 20-19N, 24W.

Doctor's office had been in the side room of a saloon. Later, when the Woodmen of the World put up a building, he secured a fine new office six feet wide and twelve feet long in back of the section for E. E. Shirley's drug store.

Doctor took a keen interest in things political and when time permitted, even at this early age, he would smoke his pipe and harangue good-naturedly with the local "experts" in such matters. In speaking many years later of some of Doctor's close friends, O. E. Null included:

"W. R. Ewing, suspected of knowing a little law became county attorney, but lost out due to spending so much time up the river at Canadian, courting the girl who became his wife. He seemed to prefer the girl to the $25 a month salary. For the past many years, Ewing has been the eminent District Judge over the Texas Panhandle.

"Charles Swindall got Ewing's job as county attorney, but abandoned the job to enter the larger field at Woodward. He became District Judge, one-time congressman and member of the state Supreme Court.

"Albert L. McRill, a dressy young Democrat came into town and was offered the job of taking over a Republican newspaper. He hesitated but needed the money. With knock-down-drag-out editorials, he drove his adversary, the other Republican newspaper out of town. On the other hand, he got along fine with the editor of the **Canadian Valley Echo,** E. L. Mitchell, a Democrat. His best job since has been city manager of Oklahoma City.

"E. L. Mitchell went from Grand to Cheyenne and took up law practice and became a District Judge and state congressman."

For some time now, he had been thinking about returning to medical school for more training. He was glad that he had not mentioned it to Della, since now that a baby was coming, it would be impossible. He would have to postpone it until a later time.

The summer passed pleasantly and on September 18, 1903, the date of their first anniversary, the baby arrived. Doctor held the healthy, squalling youngster in his arms and gazed at him in awe. His own son! The miracle of procreation and birth had impressed him deeply as a physician. Now, as a father, there were no words for his depth of feeling. They named the child Roy Ellsworth Newman, a good solid name for the son of a prominent young citizen.

On one of those rare Sunday afternoons when Doctor was spared to sit comfortably at home with his family, the subject of medical school came up

86 . . .

again. Young Roy, now twenty months old was laughing delightedly while his father jostled him on a wild bronc ride astride the doctor's foot.

"With that kind of training," Della laughed, "The boy could learn to ride a horse like old Frog. My, he was a bad animal there at first, wasn't he?"

"Those were some days," Doctor said, chuckling. "I was right out of medical school and this country looked pretty raw to compare with Ohio and Tennessee."

"Don't you think," his wife said pensively, "that we can manage somehow for you to go back for another year in medical school?"

"I have Ohio in mind when I'm ready," Doctor said. "That's pretty expensive, though, especially with a wife and child. Guess we'll have to forget it for a while."

"Yes, I know."

The citizens of Day county thought otherwise. That summer, they got busy and raised money for their doctor's tuition for a year of post-graduate work in the University of Ohio at Cincinnati. His school records accumulated and approved, he enrolled on September 18, 1905 in the Clinical and Pathological department of the university.

Meanwhile, it was discovered that they were to have another child and during mid-term, on January 20, 1906, Floyd Smith Newman was born in Doctor's old Ohio farm home.

"Are you glad it's a boy again?" Della asked her husband hopefully.

With tears in his eyes, Doctor kissed her hand and said, "A man can have no prouder possessions than sons to carry on his name."

In June, 1906, after a year's post-graduate work, Dr. Newman graduated again in medicine, from the oldest medical school west of the Allegheny Mountains and returned to practice in Grand. Doctor had promised the people of Grand that he would remain there for at least a year following graduation, for the loyalty they had shown and that he would be available even after he moved to Shattuck.

Changes were being made constantly and Doctor was aware that the railroads of the newer West played an increasingly important part in the economy and that a new era was about to open, not only here but in the entire state of Oklahoma. The Santa Fe railroad came through Shattuck, a thriving frontier town a few miles north, hauling a long string of freight cars, usually with one passenger coach at the rear. Things were on the move, and Doctor's thinking went along with the change. A young Dr. George W. Wallace, from south of the Canadian river came over with a dream of a hospital in Shattuck and the two formed a partnership, planning what was later, in 1908, to be the Northwest Sanitarium, perched on a hill in the northeast section of Shattuck.

Mesheck Haskell Newman was born on September 20, 1907, just a few weeks before the family left old Grand, and the couple's family of sons was complete. On October 30, they made the change of residence, Doctor transporting all his professional worldly effects in the back end of his buggy. It took real courage and foresight to take the chance for there was, at that time, no available house in which to live. Once more, Della's brother, Joseph (Dock) Smith came to the rescue. The Smiths had four children by that time, and the two families, of eleven people lived for two months in a small, four-room house.

Right away, Doctor secured office room in the Sears building, which he later bought and where he remained for twenty years.

Oklahoma became a state on November 16, 1907. The Constitutional Convention and the first state legislature appointed a committee to locate county seats and county boundary lines. In the first and second legislatures sat a man by the name of H. O. Tener. Back in Peebles, Ohio, Tener's brother, Charles sat down and wrote to him a special request. "When you reach Oscar Newman's county, do your best to see that he is appointed Health Commissioner." It was quite a long while before Doctor learned that his appointment had come through a boyhood friend.

Remembering the Teners, he recalled to his wife an incident which Charles Tener related many years later. "Oscar's father had working for him an old man by the name of Polly Hopkins who put out a couple of acres of watermelons and had a big crop.

"A young friend of mine drove down with me one Sunday in an old buckboard to get some watermelons. Now, old Polly was very peculiar, we learned. He would not let any of the Newman children, not even Oscar's twin brother, Edgar, step inside the watermelon patch without his express permission. That is, none except Oscar, whom he worshipped.

"So, Oscar instructed us to drive up to the west side of the patch and he proceeded to fill that old buckboard with melons. When we expressed doubt, Oscar laughed and said, 'Oh, never mind Polly. When he learns I was here, he will let on like he never missed any watermelons.' "

Another occasion of favoritism toward young Newman occurred while he was at Sewanee and he told of it to friends many times. He had put a bucket of water over a door to dump on a certain fellow when he came in. The trick worked all right, but he hadn't counted on the landlady. When someone told her they thought that O. C. Newman did it, there was another surprise. She really "blew her top" this time, declaring someone was telling a falsehood atop being destructive, for "O. C. would never, never do a thing like that."

Too, Doctor loved to recall fellow students and friends from the University of the South and what happened to them. Besides Dr. Everett S. Lain, a favorite there was Dr. Cary T. Grayson, graduated in 1903, who went on to be the personal physician of President Woodrow Wilson in the White House. And then there was one Dr. William Crawford Gorgas, who had graduated in 1875 and whose father had been president at Sewanee. Gorgas had gone on to conquer yellow fever, making possible the building of the Panama Canal and had become major-general of the United States Army.

Doctor left Grand about the time it began to diminish, and finally, to be no more. Taking away the county seat contributed to its demise and the terrible flood of 1908 did its deadly part.

Temple Houston has said of the treacherous South Canadian river at that point: "They call the Mississippi the Father of Waters. I say it would not make a ramrod for this son-of-a-gun."

The mighty river swelled its banks along the north shore and Horse Shoe Bend began to fall away and be carried off with the turbulent flood. All the farmers along that rim suffered more or less, but the greatest loser was Hyram Walck, known as Hi Walck, who was, ironically, the founder of Grand. His was doubtless the richest and most progressive farm in the county. One evening, the farm was there and the next morning when the sun came up, it was gone, washed toward the sea.

CHAPTER VII

EARLY DAYS AT SHATTUCK

The little red pump house was one of the most important spots in town. George Busch had come here when there was no town to speak of, and proudly took over the pump house for the Atchison, Topeka and Santa Fe railroad. The little building housed the steam engine that pumped water for operating the trains. The engine was George Busch's pride and joy, with its brass bands which Busch kept shining like a diamond. The pumper led a lonely life withal, making only an occasional trip to Kiowa, Kansas for groceries.

In the intervening years, the town grew up around the railroad trade. The town site had been formed in 1901 by a company from Missouri, and May Daniel was the first child born here. T. N. Miller was the first postmaster and merchant and his wife was the first school teacher in Shattuck, receiving forty dollars a month for teaching 33 pupils on a first grade certificate examination taken at Woodward. Pastor T. A. Butler preached for $4 a month at the Baptist church on Main street.

Indians camped along Rock creek, killing every dog they could lure, and young cattle when the opportunity afforded, jerking the meat and calling it venison.

Prohibition was voted with statehood, but the town was wide open with a half dozen saloons, several gambling halls and a house of prostitution, unappropriately called the "White House." From First street to the railroad tracks was a real red light district, but some of it was cleaned out shortly, including the house of ill fame. Having all the earmarks of a frontier settlement on the border of No Man's Land, early Shattuck was rough and tough. Men would congregate in gang fights around the saloons and spend several days in this pitched battle before finally tiring and going home.

From two blocks, the town grew to four, and in 1905, the Sears addition gave a boost. Billy Sears, the town mayor, established the Shattuck Realty company and the boom was on. This town was the only shipping point north to the Kansas line and for many miles in the other directions. Freight wagons pulled by eight and ten mules or horses swarmed into Shattuck for supplies shipped in by railway. This business demanded feed yards, and in 1905, a half dozen such yards were in operation on a grand scale.

The feed yards consisted of a large, fenced-in corral with stables and a hay mow near the entrance gate. Attached to the barn would be a long shed with mangers and stalls. Opposite was the bunk house where the teamsters stayed overnight. Equipment furnished was a cook stove, a crude table and benches, two or three skillets and some empty, gallon syrup pails to be used for making coffee. The cowpunchers would pile in at any hour, make coffee and bed down in their own bed roll on the floor.

George Mason had a first rate livery stable which he sold to George Brown, who also owned a classy hotel and rooming house. Paul Barcafer ran the Earl hotel which figured prominently in the life of Shattuck.

A frequent sight in the early days were herds of wild horses, driven in from the plains of Arizona, New Mexico and Texas by horse traders. The animals were commonly mustangs, or descendants of the wild Spanish horses, wiry, tough and unkempt. Many were later broken out for useful saddle animals or gentle buggy horses. At times, beautiful and mild mannered gentle horses were found running with the wild steeds.

Cattle were driven overland to the railroad station for shipping to Eastern markets which meant Shattuck required a large stockyard. This too, furnished business and made a profit. Droves of cattle on the trail or road held the right of way, by frontier law.

The growing cow town had a hardware store, run by T. N. Young, as well as saddle and harness shops. Several blacksmith shops provided wagon wheel repair and horse shoeing.

Broom corn thrived on the sod and this was known to be the largest broom corn market in the world. In season, baled broom corn was piled for blocks approaching the railroad station. Cotton was a little less successful, but a good crop, and two cotton gins were necessary in Shattuck.

Merchants to set up business included the Patterson Brothers, Jacob Weber, Fred Becker and George Schultz, the latter three married to sisters. One other merchant in general merchandise business was C. C. Weiss. George Schultz, a naturalized

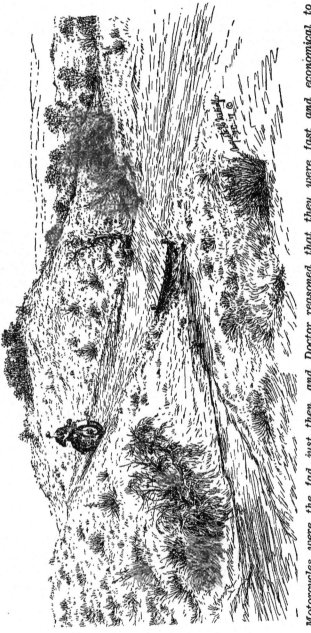

Motorcycles were the fad just then, and Doctor reasoned that they were fast and economical to keep up so he purchased a single-cylinder, belt drive Harley-Davidson.

citizen who helped to bring many of his countrymen to the new West, paid their passage and lent financial aid until they were settled. Those citizens formed the backbone of Shattuck business in later years.

A sprinkler wagon hauled water and dribbled it over the deep dust of the streets. Main street was up hill and down, with a few plank sidewalks above the deep mud or dust of the thoroughfare. Each business house had a porch, with a steep flight of steps and a platform leading from hitching post to veranda. A large windmill and water tank stood in the center of town.

John Barcafer drove the hack, which looked much like an old-time stagecoach to meet "drummers" as they arrived by train, and take them to the hotels. O. G. Gibbs ran a milk wagon and those who didn't own a cow or goat could buy milk at their doors in their own buckets or pans for five cents a quart. "Slaughter House Mike" drove from his spread to town behind a team of oxen, and once at a community picnic, the Indians held a sham battle and burned his wagon. Four dray lines, operated by O. R. Miller, O. H. James, D. Weire and Bud Snowden, were all kept busy.

Outside the city limits at West Rock creek crossing stood a huge cottonwood tree known far and near as a landmark. Weary travelers, upon seeing the top of the cottonwood, knew they were almost to Shattuck. Early treaties had been signed there, many an early day trader there lost his bank roll to a card shark; picnic parties were frequent at the cottonwood and it is said that many marriage matches were made in its benevolent shade. Circuit rider preachers here converted folk to Christianity and baptized them in nearby brisk and bubbling Rock creek.

This was the Shattuck to which Doctor brought his family in the historic year of 1907, there to live until his death nearly a half century later, and to become, himself, a legend.

After two months with the Smiths, the doctor's family found a little two-room house in Shattuck which was home for the ensueing two years, after which they bought the location which was to be home for the rest of his life.

Before the good physician decided on traveling by car, he went in for motorcycles, which were the fad just then. Doctor reasoned that they were fast and economical to keep up. So he purchased a single cylinder, belt-drive Harley-Davidson. Learning to ride it was equally as bad as the taming of Frog and perhaps more dangerous. The people of Shattuck who were concerned for his welfare shook their heads and wondered if, rather than an advance in his mode of travel, perhaps this was a step backward.

Bob Denney was one of the veteran motorcycle riders who teamed up with others to teach Doctor to conquer the bucking machine. On Sunday afternoons and late evenings, they would take him out for trial runs. After a particularly bad spill one evening, Doctor led the demon into S. A. Gibson's repair shop. The repairman looked it over and asked, "Why don't you run that piece of junk up into a fence corner and leave it?"

Doctor chuckled and rubbed a couple of bruises.

98 . . .

"Oh, I don't know," he said. "A man's got to get around fast in this day and time."

Doctor got his motorcycle across the river many times. A. G. Carver, who lived at Durham on the opposite side of the South Canadian used to watch for him when there was a call in those parts, and help him across. Carver's children, a girl of nine (later Mrs. Frank Kolander) and other brothers and sisters would note when someone fell ill, then race pell mell to the river side and watch for the roaring motorcycle and Doctor, with his coat-tails flapping in the wind. The youngsters would wave at him and Doctor never failed to wave back.

At last, Doctor was knocked unconscious in a spill while attempting to get his motorcycle past a team of wild horses, so he abandoned the machine in favor of a new Flanders automobile. Sometime later, he had an EMF car. Asked one time what the initials EMF meant, Doctor replied promptly and with a perfectly straight face: "Every morning fix."

William Sears, the realtor, Ben Smith, a farmer and Dr. L. T. Green were partners with the founders of the Northwest Sanitarium and all were very disappointed that it failed almost from the start.

Dr. Newman's patient wife never questioned him about how the hospital was coming along, knowing that if he felt like discussing it, he knew that she was always there with a sympathetic ear and an understanding heart. But it was not long until she could see that the people were not supporting their hospital and thus, depriving themselves of a life-saving opportunity.

"Why can't people understand?" Doctor asked her one evening, following a late supper and after the little boys were in bed. "They have their sicknesses, their operations and their babies, but they simply will not come to the hospital. Why?"

"They believe in you, dear," Mrs. Newman said. "Have you tried explaining all this to patients in a way they can understand?"

Doctor sighed deeply. "For once, I can't seem to get through to anyone, no matter how I approach the subject. Well, it looks as if we'll have to pull in our belts another notch. You know that I've gone heavily in debt for the hospital." He put an arm about her shoulders and smoothed her dark hair. "It hurts me, Della, to see you and the boys suffer and I know I can't give you more than the bare necessities to exist on. For myself, I don't mind."

"It's all for the best," Della assured him. "Things will come out all right. Just have faith and don't you worry."

Doctor's office was one half block north of the Earl hotel. The idea of maintaining in Shattuck a well-equipped hospital was frequently discussed in the lobby of the hotel by the more progressive, thinking people. Weary and discouraged, Doctor would often stop in late at night and "talk hospital" with Paul Barcafer, who, as a patient, had been in and out of a good many hospitals.

The problem of furnishing the Northwest Sanitarium had been a problem at the outset. Old friends and business associates made contributions. John Barcafer was running the picture show and he ran

100 . . .

all pictures as benefits for a couple of weeks, money collected going for hospital furnishings. And all to no avail.

After the Northwest Sanitarium closed for lack of patients and funds, the nurse, Dora McIntosh came along to Shattuck from Grand and opened her father's home of four rooms for a cottage hospital. Mr. McIntosh obliged by driving on calls. On lengthy trips, Doctor would sleep, and the bumpy cow trails never seemed to disturb his exhausted body as he napped. At one time, there was an emergency call to Follett, Texas and McIntosh got the doctor there in the tin lizzie in time to save a life, though it meant driving through a couple of gates without opening them.

The nearest hospital now was in Wichita, Kansas and Doctor was the only surgeon over a very large area. Registered nurses were simply not to be had at first, trained and practical nurses came from among neighborhood women who were willing to be taught by Dr. Newman. Mrs. Mary Booth was one of the women available for helping to deliver babies, always in the homes, and Mrs. A. M. Garringer was another who specialized in OB cases. To name them all might require pages. Often, the only fuel for heat was damp broom corn seed and the only water was secured by melting snow in vessels on the stove during the winter, or carrying it from neighbor's wells, or the town well.

Surgery was performed in homes, also. Doctor had the family of a patient to remove from one room all furniture and if they had them, rugs and curtains. The floors were sprinkled with water and all instruments sterilized on a portable sterilizer set on the kitchen stove.

Bob Denney and Fred Teeten sold the doctor a kerosene pressure burner to be used for sterilizing instruments, but getting it to generate was often a problem. These two men were on call day or night to coax service from the pressure burner.

One cold, windy night about two a.m., Doctor called Denney. There was an emergency and the burner wouldn't go. The serviceman got the contraption operating and Doctor apologized for getting him out of his warm bed at such an unearthly hour, adding that he felt he should be compensated.

"No," Denney replied. "We sold it, and its up to us to make it work."

"Tell you what," Doctor said seriously. "If you'll stick around while they're getting the patient ready, I'll take out your appendix." Needless to relate, the man kept his appendix.

Preparing an operating room in the home required some four hours of work. When all was ready, the folding operating table was set up, the patient anesthetized, and the surgery proceeded under ordinary light. Often, Doctor would do the greater part, then have the nurse finish off the minor details under his direction. He was an excellent teacher of medicine, but always knew when and where to step in, himself. When the operation was completed, the bed was moved into the room where the patient stayed during convalescence.

By the following year after the Newman's arrival, a telephone exchange was established by O. H. James and son in their own residence.

Also, in 1908, a disasterous fire occurred and two blocks of Shattuck were destroyed. Every possible wagon, buggy and hack hauled barrels of water from Rock creek which was dashed by bucketsful on the licking flames. Nearby roofs were covered with flour, sand and salt but the destruction spread until halted by a stone building owned and occupied by Northrup Jewelry. The town then decided to buy fire equipment, so a team of horses and a fire wagon were placed in charge of Oscar Barnett. Soon, the horses were so well trained that they were off at the first blast of the whistle.

The people continued to keep Doctor constantly on call, often as not without being able ever to pay, and he never refused a call whatever the weather or distance, and regardless of how much sleep he had lost or how he felt. During an epidemic of influenza, he went day and night. Whole families would be in bed and Doctor would double as errand boy wherever he could. At one home, everyone in the family except the mother was sick and after ministering to their needs and leaving medicine for which they could not pay, he picked up the milk buckets, went to the barn and milked several cows by hand before leaving.

Doctor appreciated every little favor and acknowledged it in one way or another. Children, especially, liked him and he adored them in return. In the Getz home, he called on Mrs. Getz and during the examination, he noticed that the eight-year-old girl, Byrdie, hurried from the room and the noise of clattering pots and pans began in the kitchen. When he had finished with the patient and was about to depart, Byrdie rushed in and wrapped her small arms about him. "No, please, don't go yet. I've cooked dinner for you."

Immensely flattered, the great man sat down to a nice meal and "some of the best biscuits I ever ate."

In one way, Dr. Newman was like a child in that he could hardly take his own medicine. He rarely became actually ill, but on one occasion, he said to his associate, Dr. Rollo: "Jimmy, I don't know what I'm going to do. I feel awful."

"Ha, I can fix that. You're going to take castor oil," the doctor declared, uncorking a big bottle of the thick, foul-tasting medicine.

"Oh, no!" Doctor insisted. "You know I can't swallow that stuff."

Doctor Newman and his associate, Dr. J. W. Rollo, in the Shattuck office in the year 1924.

"Sure you can. Every little child that gets sick has to take castor oil, remember?" So Dr. Rollo fixed him a dose and made him take it.

Doctor's generosity manifested itself in many ways. He was quick to lend a boost to young, deserving people who were having difficulty getting ahead. One of these persons was a struggling young lawyer, Ben F. Barnett. Doctor, always interested in honest politics, recommended Barnett for county judge of the newly formed Ellis county, a position he held for twenty years, until his death.

After Dr. Newman's financial difficulties were behind, he sponsored the medical education of one of the Smith youngsters, his wife's nephew, who became Dr. J. J. Smith, obstetrician and surgeon and who affiliated with his uncle's hospital permanently after going to pre-med at McMurry College and graduating from George Washington university in St. Louis. If the number of boys who became physicians as the result of Doctor's direct encouragement were known, it would be an impressive list, and the same applies to his inspiration to girls who later entered the nursing profession.

But back in early Shattuck, Doctor enjoyed the silent pictures as soon as they made their appearance in this country, and went as often as he could get away from duty. However, he rarely could see the ending of a movie, and many people have wondered if he ever saw a complete story on the screen from beginning to end. Inevitably, the picture would be shut off and a voice would inquire: "Is Dr. Newman in the house?" and out Doctor would go, carrying his black bag.

The first air dome theater was called the

Nickelodeon; the flickers were accompanied by elaborate piano effects, and admission price was five cents for adults, children free. Traveling troupes brought plays here annually; and the leading citizens of Shattuck presented many home talent plays, such as "Uncle Tom's Cabin" and "Ten Nights in a Bar Room." Any person in town who could play an instrument was welcome in the Shattuck Band which played regular Saturday night concerts.

This was the Shattuck that Oscar Newman loved and made his own. In return, Oscar Newman belonged to Shattuck.

CHAPTER VIII

GOOD TIMES AND BAD

A blizzard howled dismally across the plains country and the snowdrifts deepened. Business had slowed almost to a standstill, but as usual, Doctor's work had increased with the inclement weather. Over on Commission creek, twenty-five miles southwest, the time came for the delivery of a baby and Doctor was summoned to hurry.

"Get out the car, John," Doctor said to young Barcafer. "We'll have to get there."

"Through these drifts? We'll never make it."

"Take a good strong scoop. We're on our way."

John put in a long handled straight spade for digging off high centers and a wide scoop for moving snow. They cut across fields and pastures, scooping snow at fence lines. Doctor had not been to bed for thirty-six hours, and when they would get stuck, John noticed that it seemed to please him. He would just slide down in the coyote fur coat he was wearing and sleep until the young man dug out. When they started to move again, Doctor would light up a smoke and stare moodily through the front of the tin lizzie.

Six hours later, they reached their destination. Helping the doctor get his bag from the car, John said, "You'd better charge these people plenty,

Doctor had not been to bed for thirty-six hours, and when they would get stuck, he simply smuggled down in his coyote fur coat and slept until John dug out.

because I'm going to charge you by the ton for all the snow I've shovelled."

Doctor chuckled at the joke, then his face sobered. "John, that was sure a hard trip for you all right, and you can charge accordingly, but these folks are as poor as church mice and I can't charge them anything."

They were just in time for delivery of a baby and John Barcafer didn't charge a dime for the trip. People were like that around Doctor; he somehow brought out the best in their natures by the inspiration of his own unselfish dedication to service.

Doctor bought an automobile some time later from S. Q. Gibson, a Flanders Twenty. Top speed down hill for the Flanders was some thirty miles an hour, and Doctor "allowed" that it was perhaps so new, that it was not yet perfected, since it was broken down most of the time. If a call took him very far, it was necessary to get Gibson's chief mechanic to go along and drive so that repairs could be made on the way. The mechanic's name was Rosy Sears, and he was a whiz with automobiles.

Natives of Shattuck and surrounding country, as Doctor and Rosy chugged by, would chant: "You can always tell by the sound of the gears, that the man at the throttle is Rosy Sears."

Doctor decided later that he preferred to do his own driving, especially after he got into the Buick line with the dealer, V. F. Wilson, but meanwhile, many men had the novel and unforgettable experience of driving Dr. Newman on calls.

Dr. O. C. being the only surgeon in the region, medical doctors in other towns tried to arrange, when possible, to have several operations done in one trip when they sent to Shattuck for Doctor to come to their town.

On one occasion, after a heavy snowfall, he headed for Canadian, Texas, taking along Louise Cramer, who was his superintendent of nurses and Opal Booth Karn, a registered nurse. The road east of Higgins was drifted full and they had to be towed for some distance several times. The three ate a hot, noon meal with Dr. Caldwell and his wife, relaxed for a few minutes, then started operating. That afternoon, Doctor performed a Caesarian section, a hemorrhoidectomy and four tonsillectomies before hitting the drifts for the return home, Doctor driving despite his fatigue. Arriving in Shattuck about ten p.m., he took the nurses home, then made his hospital rounds, though late, before going home to retire.

Doctor had to get along without an incubator for premature babies in the earlier days of his hospital practice, but he fought gallantly to keep life in the tiny infants. Placing a piece of gauze over the child's mouth, he would breathe into it's lungs. He taught several of his various nurses, one of them Opal Booth, the art of breathing correctly to start the process in a newborn. The nurse would take over temporarily while Doctor got his own breath and rested a minute. Great drops of perspiration stood on his face as he worked, until at length, the little one could fill his lungs with oxygen and scream life into his tiny body.

Doctor had a faithful collie dog which had a habit of following and running ahead or behind the

110 . . .

car. So long as the calls were nearby, the doctor didn't mind, but on long trips, he would try all kinds of shenanigans to get away from the dog.

Quite by accident one day, he learned the foolproof way to do it. He came rattling by the Barcafer home near the north end of Main street with the dog following and barking. John's bull dog, Rounder, made a mad dash and jumped out the collie away from the car and back around the block. The collie cut down the alley in an attempt to catch his master's car, but the bull dog came back down Main and headed him off at the next intersection. By then, Doctor, enjoying himself immensely, had gone out of sight and the collie, tongue drooping, trotted back home.

If the citizens wondered where Doctor was going when he started on a call, they could get an idea whether it was far or near by observing whether he headed for Barcafer's in his little game to get rid of the dog.

One of Doctor's favorite foods was roasting ears of corn, boiled on the cob, and he would eat several ears at a sitting—"about the average you'd feed a hard-working mule." Another food of which he was fond was onions, preferably raw. "I eat onions every time I can lay hands on them," he told an associate. "I eat them in self-defense. When examining patients, if they aren't careful with their breath, I retaliate in kind."

One night, Charlotte Kuntz was sitting up with a neighbor's eight-year-old boy who was suffering with pneumonia. Doctor came in at near midnight to check the child's condition.

"Doctor, you look exhausted," Charlotte observed. "Have you had supper?"

"Not tonight," Doctor said.

"Then I'll get you something warm."

"If I may have exactly what I want," Doctor insisted, "I'd like a glass of milk, buttered bread and an onion." He ate it heartily and was again on his way.

The Northwest Sanitarium, established in 1908, was doomed to failure and with its fall, Doctor suffered financial reverses that took several years to overcome. But no one ever heard him complain, nor did his wife or young sons. Rather, they cheerfully shared what they had, wherever it was needed. Sick and suffering people came into town from long distances, and having no money with which to stay at a hotel, they went directly to Doctor's home, where Mrs. Newman cooked and served their meals as guests while they received medical treatment for which many could never hope to pay. Nor did most of them entertain any illusions that they could.

Doctor returned to private practice and plugged along as best he could. Gentle Della sent the boys to school and kept things going efficiently at home, as economically as was possible. Her husband tried to leave work and anxiety on the doorstep when he came home, and she never brought up the subject. If he cared to talk, she listened. If he chose to spend an entire evening in absolute silence, she quietly acquiesced. The boys adored their father, "worshipped" would be more nearly descriptive of their feelings. A few kind words or a clasp of his hand on their shoulders, out of his preoccupation, was enough to put them in a contented glow for days.

In 1913, the Newmans scraped together enough for Doctor to spend two weeks of training in newer surgical methods at the famous Mayo Clinic in Rochester, Minnesota. From that year until the time of his death, he spent from three to six weeks at Mayo's, thirty-two times in all. The science and advance of medicine was virtually a religion to Oscar C. Newman. Interspersed with these sessions were many others to Chicago and Ohio; he spent some time every year in the pursuit of further medical knowledge through post-graduate work in institutions especially equipped for the purpose.

Doctor's advance in Masonry continued, with his Blue Lodge membership now being in Joppa Lodge No. 262 at Shattuck. He occupied the chair of Senior Warden in 1911 and that of Worshipful Master in 1912. That year, he continued his search for further enlightenment in Masonry by taking the 4th through 32nd degrees in the Oklahoma consistory at Guthrie. At this time, he was initiated into the Shrine and became a member of India Temple at Oklahoma City. It might be said here that O. C. was the only one of the Newman brothers to follow their father's steps in taking the degrees of Masonry.

James Tuthill was Doctor's office boy from 1914 to 1917, doing such tasks as sweeping out the office, dusting the furniture and keeping the doctor's new Model T roadster filled with gas and rarin' to go.

That first year, young Tuthill learned about the

hardships Doctor took as a matter of course, when he was asked to drive on a call twelve miles north of Shattuck. As usual, Dr. O. C. slept most of the way but was instantly alert when they arrived on call. The driver waited several hours while Doctor made a delivery and they reached home around one a.m.

"I don't see how you do it, day after day," the young man observed when Doctor let him out at home.

"I'll just drop around by the office," Doctor yawned.

Young Tuthill learned the following morning that the doctor had found an emergency call waiting that night to go south of Arnett. Thinking it would be too much to ask his youthful driver to go out again, Doctor went alone, and in crossing the South Canadian on the return trip, he got stuck and did not return to town until late that afternoon. He and the car were plastered with mud all over, and Doctor was exhausted, having been up and at work almost two days and nights, most of it without food.

Doctor confessed to dozing while driving alone; in later years, at goodly speeds, but was always fortunate in that it never incurred an accident. Even when visiting with friends, he would doze momentarily, but without missing anything from the conversation.

Attention to his patients was, however, another thing. However exhausted, he was responsive to their needs. His nurses would see him sit down in a hard, straight backed chair and be almost instantly asleep. He depended upon the nurse to watch, and at one word, he was on the job.

World War I came along and on June 21, 1918, Dr. O. C. Newman was appointed First Lieutenant in the Medical Section of the Officer's Reserve Corps and hustled off to Camp McArthur in Waco, Texas. Mrs. Newman had just had surgery and the boys were young for responsibility at home, Roy, the oldest having reached just fifteen. But, characteristic of him, Doctor did not have a comment about the turn of events, just began to get ready to go.

He made calls as late as possible on the day he left, and many people had been paying on their accounts. Late that evening, just a few minutes before train time, Doctor rushed by the Kuntz' store, emptied his pockets of money and checks, and told his friends: "Count it and put it in the bank for me tomorrow, will you?" And out he raced to catch his train.

In military camp, Doctor found his immediate superiors to be "little upstarts just out of medical school." For once in his life, he resented members of his own profession, these fledglings whose judgment in medicine was poor from inexperience, but who would not listen to the voice of experience. To Doctor, welfare of the patient was still the important thing.

When the terrible flu epidemic of 1918 visited its scourge, Dr. Newman and his orderlies were in charge of five hundred soldiers. Daily, they dropped like flies, and Doctor worked the longest and hardest hours of his life, meanwhile suffering a mild case of flu himself. Of all the men on the ground, he did not lose one case. However, among his men who were hospitalized, he had no further word.

Mrs. Newman went down to see him once, and upon returning home, she brought as a gift an army uniform "just like Dad's" to fit the smallest boy, Haskell. The little fellow, now eleven years old, was the proudest boy in town, as he paraded all over to show the neighbors his "army suit."

During August, when the Texas plains were unbearably hot, dry and dusty, a soldier was stricken ill on the field. Doctor was by his side instantly, making a hasty examination.

"You!" he snapped to the man at his elbow. "Bring a pail of water, and be quick about it."

The order was carried out on the double. The water-carrier was Doctor's colonel.

Capt. O. C. Newman, Mr. Wilson, W. E. Stuart, standing unknown, J. W. Foster

116 . . .

The people of Shattuck, left now without medical care, petitioned directly to Washington with the signatures of virtually every man, woman and child in Ellis county, for the return of their doctor from the army. The petition was granted and Doctor was honorably discharged from active service on December 7, 1918. On February 7, 1919, he was made chairman of the Military Training Camps association of the United States, in Ellis county, Oklahoma.

Things began to change for the better after Doctor returned from the army. Time had changed the attitude of many oldtimers concerning the benefits of an organized hospital, and the younger generation had been in favor of such facilities from the beginning. He came home with good plans for reopening the hospital on his own as soon as possible. He became so intent with these plans that he once forgot that he had five hundred bushels of wheat, raised by a tenant, in an elevator at Higgins.

Perpetually harassed by overwork and the demands upon his time and energy, Doctor was nonetheless of smooth, even temperament, totally without hostility. His gift for listening was perhaps his greatest attribute as a physician. Everyone wanted to talk to him personally, and by doing so, were frequently cured of their ailments, even in a day before psychoanalysis was generally recognized. Patients felt that they could relate their ailments and if Doctor was not perceptibly aroused, there was nothing serious about their condition, and they would be all right. If there was any reason for treatment, Doctor did so, promptly.

Whether or not the doctor heard everything the patient was saying, at least the patient thought so. There was something so homely and homespun about him that the individual felt completely at ease in his presence. Many people have wondered, and associates have pondered the secret of Doctor's gift and a few discovered for themselves that it had something to do with love, for Dr. Newman loved every living thing, especially human beings.

The doctor could prepare his patients for any emergency, quietly and unobtrusively. Cecil Henson had had surgery and Doctor was visiting with him some ten days after the operation. They discussed the type of incision and surgery Cecil had undergone. Doctor spoke of some of the complications that sometimes followed that type, and went on to say that methods had been developed to take care of such an emergency.

"I never suspected," Henson said, years later, "That he was preparing me to meet these same complications within twenty-four hours. Thanks to his wisdom and tact, there was no worry or fear on my part when it happened, and I made a complete recovery."

Doctor had a way of freeing his patients from that old killer, Fear. This was his greatest prescription. When it seemed indicated, Dr. O. C. would discuss with his patients the place God held in the life of man. His favorite story along this line concerned a man who had been bedfast for a number of years and who remarked one day to Doctor: "You know, I've done a lot of church-going and attended a lot of protracted meetings, but I've learned more about God here on this old bed than all of them put together."

118 . . .

Incurable diseases were grievous to him and a constant challenge. Of infantile paralysis, he said: "When they discover the cause, they will find that the germ is carried by a fly."

One of his early patients, while still associated with Dr. Green, was a young girl named Luviele Patterson who suffered from epilepsy. He never led the father, John Wilsie Patterson or any of the family to believe that she would ever be well, but sought constantly, year after year, for something to lessen the severity of her convulsions.

In the fall of 1916, Doctor had a serious operation involving a crushed skull which rested on the brain. Once again, the patient came from the Patterson family, a small boy of six called Jack (Floyd) who was hit by a twelve-pound shot-put ball made of iron.

There was no hospital and Doctor promised himself that if this child survived a home operation, he would redouble his efforts to give the next such emergency a better chance for survival. Doctor called in Dr. Tedrowe from Woodward and Dr. Silverthorne of Waynoka, and a room in the home was prepared for the operating table. The home physician thought that one of the older doctors should operate, but the family wanted their own doctor, so the others stood by to assist if necessary. The boy survived delicate brain surgery in a four hour ordeal and later graduated from high school with honors at age fifteen.

Doctor marvelled ever afterward at what he gained in experience and confidence by that one operation.

In 1920, the original Shattuck Hospital was opened.

CHAPTER IX

The Hospital

In 1920, the old hospital, known a dozen years earlier as the Northwest Sanitarium, was reopened. At last, the public was ready to support and accept the benefits of a hospital, and Doctor was sure of himself this time.

Having trained good medical assistants from the raw material of his own acquaintances, Doctor never had much difficulty in this respect. Goldie Wilson has been, through the years, a part of the Newman institution. He hired her as his office nurse after his return from service in 1919. Doctor employed Goldie one day at noon just as he was about to leave town on a call.

"There's just one thing I want you to keep in mind," he told her. "I want to always be able to depend on what you say."

Goldie gave that statement a little thought. Why should she ever want to lie to Dr. Newman, of all people! As time went on, she saw occasions when a little fib might have made things a bit easier; such as the morning when she was just about to leave on vacation and in her hurry and excitement, broke three hypodermic syringes. But she remained utterly honest with Doctor and is to this day with the Shattuck hospital and clinic.

"Where shall I begin?" Goldie asked Doctor that first day.

"Just look around and find where everything is," he told her. "I must be on my way now, but I'll be back as soon as I can."

The new office nurse did not see him until afternoon of the following day, but she "found everything" and has ever since known where everything is.

Goldie adored Doctor, but she often became indignant for what she thought was unfairness toward him by patients. She had not been with him long when he was called into the country during a spell of rain and deep mud. When he had almost reached his destination, the car became hopelessly stuck. The patient's husband furnished horsepower for pulling the car from the mire, and in the struggle, a singletree belonging to the farmer was broken. When they settled the bill, the farmer charged Doctor for the singletree and Goldie could never forget it.

Again, she used to take him to task for depriving himself of much payment for services rendered. Upon sending out statements, she has seen people come in to pay, but, with money in hand, Doctor would have them take it back, declaring there was nothing owing. This occurred many times when Doctor knew that the family was in need.

He was patient with mistakes of his staff of employees. Goldie frequently took him the wrong patient's record and he would find a woman with prostatic trouble, or a man who had had an ovary removed.

122 . . .

On one occasion, Goldie was about to go on vacation and Doctor sent her word not to leave town until she saw him. He asked if she had plenty of money and she confessed to having twenty dollars. "I want you to have a good time," he said, giving her all the money in his pockets except the change.

One of his jokes to her was, "Pull up a chair and let's smoke for about an hour."

Louise Cramer was another long-time member of the staff, acting as superintendent of nurses for thirty years. She was never married, devoting her whole life to her work. She took a proprietary interest in the doctor's sons, their education and growing enthusiasm for medical professions, and could not resist "bossing" them. Once she said to an associate: "If I had not been so bossy, I would have had a husband." But she would not have had her life and career otherwise.

When the first son started off to college, Doctor joked, "I'm trying to wean Roy from the pocket-book," but he never skimped on giving them every opportunity.

The patronage at the hospital increased and in 1927, a thirty-nine-room fireproof building was erected and named the Shattuck Hospital. Two years later, twenty-six more rooms were added. With every expansion, one rule was observed: Dr. Newman would have no wards. "Even poor folks appreciate a private room," he declared.

Roy, Floyd and Haskell were earnest in their considerations for careers, and only in one exception did they think of being other than doctors. At one time, Floyd thought that he would enjoy putting his mathematical bent to being an accountant, but the idea did not last long and he, too, pursued the study of medicine.

To gentle Della Newman, their decisions were the reward of her hopes and subtle guidance. Doctor often referred to her as "the power behind the throne" which resulted in the blessing of physician sons and, more happily, sons who returned to join their father's staff.

Roy went to the University of Oklahoma where he received his Bachelor of Arts degree. Here, he fell in love with Virginia Gossett whose home was in Bolckow, Missouri and the two were married on September 27, 1928.

All his preparation for the practice of medicine lay ahead, and he decided upon the medical department of Baylor university in Dallas, Texas. Roy graduated with the degree of Doctor of Medicine in 1932. He subsequently studied at Cook county Postgraduate Medical School in Chicago, Washington University, in St. Louis, and the Mayo Clinic. His chosen specialties were Pediatrics (diseases of children), Orthopedics (correction and prevention of deformities, especially in children) and Cardiology (diagnosis and treatment of diseases of the heart.) Dr. Roy served his interneship at the Missouri Methodist Hospital in St. Joseph, Missouri.

Not having children of their own, Roy and Virginia adopted a small girl and named her Patsy Ann. On her first arrival at the home of her new grandaddy, of whom she grew particularly fond, Patsy Ann was asked by Doctor: "And who are you?"

Without hestitation, she piped: "I'm a New-man."

Floyd attended his freshman year at the University of Oklahoma then went to the Westminister College for Men at Fulton, Missouri for the next two terms. Two years of pre-medical training followed at Baylor then he went to the medical school of the University of Tennessee, at Memphis, graduating with the degree of Medical Doctor in December, 1931. He served a year's interneship at the Muhlenberg Hospital in Plainview, New Jersey, then took a six-month postgraduate course at Columbia University in New York, a two-month course in New Orleans and another in Chicago.

Dr. Floyd's specialty is in diseases of the eye, ear, nose and throat. He was a Major in the Army during World War II and in February, 1949 was married to Erwina Schollenbarger. They have two children, Robert and Ruth Ann.

Haskell went to Westminister College for Men for two years, followed by two years of pre-medical at Baylor University. He graduated with his medical degree from the University of Tennessee in 1932.

Meanwhile, Haskell had married a Mississippi miss, Cornelia Bridges on September 29, 1929. The same year he received his MD, JoAnn was born, and Haskell jr. arrived in 1937. There followed two years of interneship in Duvall county hospital, a charity institution in Jacksonville, Florida. At the age of thirty-three, Dr. Haskell received his Fellowship in the American College of Surgeons. His specialty is in Urology (diseases of the kidneys and related organs) and general surgery.

While the sons were away at school there was, among other members of Doctor's staff, a favorite, Dr. John P. Davis. Doctor had suffered an attack of acute nephritis in the spring of 1929 and it became obvious that he would need a close assistant. Dr. Davis, then practicing in Arnett, had been to the Shattuck Hospital several times where he consulted with Doctor about surgical instruments.

Dr. Newman drove down to Arnett one day and in an interview, he asked Davis about becoming his partner and on what terms he might come to Shattuck. The partnership was formed and Dr. Davis thus received immediate prestige over a wide area.

But still, the people demanded Dr. Newman for examinations, and Dr. Davis, as junior partner, was not able to relieve him of as much work as he would have liked to have done. Davis did the numerous other things at the hospital and learned a very great deal from the older man. Between the two developed a fine friendship that lasted the rest of Doctor's lifetime.

The years of Dr. Davis' association with Doctor, 1929 to 1935 were depression years, and western Oklahoma was in a dust bowl. About the close of this time, Doctor had charged off more than $200,000 worth of unpaid doctor bills, remembering them no more against the people of the area.

One incident that Dr. Davis never forgot, however, was the well-to-do but stingy man who came in with numerous and bizarre complaints. The patient was sure that there was something seriously wrong with every system and organ of his body. He demanded minute examination, and Doctor spent two hours going over him carefully and making X-rays and every known laboratory test.

Finally, the patient was putting on his clothes and about to take his departure when he looked Doctor squarely in the eye and said, in all seriousness: "Now Doc, I don't owe you nothin', do I?"

Dr. Davis related a case of pseudo-psiesis which Doctor handled in his town and which was one of his strangest cases. A woman of thirty-eight had suffered sterility and at last came to Doctor with the announcement that she was now expecting a child. She had missed several menstrual periods and pregnancy looked possible. However, after thorough examination, Doctor turned to the husband and said, "Well, your wife is not pregnant."

The woman was indignant and would not believe the diagnosis. Month after month, she returned, and the diagnosis remained the same, not expectant. Nevertheless, the patient's abdomen grew larger all the time. At the end of what the woman calculated to be the gestation period, she went to bed with various and sundry pains and after a few hours of this "labor," Doctor was summoned.

He gave her another examination and called the husband to one side. "I'm awfully sorry," he said, "But this woman is not going to have a baby."

"Then how do you explain her size?"

"Frankly, she suffers from a little gas on the stomach and a very great deal of plain fat. Her own thinking has resulted in this more than two hundred pounds of weight."

Soon after, the patient resumed her monthly periods.

In those days, Doctor operated on an average of four to five hundred major surgical cases a year and an equal number of minor procedures. In August, he reaped a harvest of tonsils, when he would do from sixty to a hundred cases a month, using the Sleuder instrument. Dr. Davis' three-year-old son was one of these cases, and the young man administered the ether with much fear and trembling.

With a heavy obstetrical practice and seeing perhaps a dozen other patients for every surgical case, Doctor worked long hours, rarely leaving the hospital before ten at night.

Ellis county had then some 7,500 people, 1,500 of them living in Shattuck. But the patients streamed in from a hundred or more miles away. After the sons returned and facilities were expanded, as many as fifty patients were seen in an afternoon, not counting those who had waited all morning. As many as fifteen towns were represented in any half day, some people passing seventeen doctors to get there.

Goldie's pet peeve was people saying, "Goldie, are you here?" As if she would be any place else!

Doctor was a stickler for neatness, wearing a spotless shirt with a detachable collar which was somewhat low and comfortable-looking. A forehand tie was tucked in the bosom of his shirt. He wore excellent suits, well pressed, and his shoes were always shined.

He ate lunch at the hospital except on Sunday, when Mrs. Newman prepared an elaborate meal, after which Doctor relaxed for a couple of hours unless an emergency called him back to duty. Supper was usually past eight o'clock, and he always returned to the hospital afterward for final rounds and to see late stragglers, sometimes a roomful of them.

During these years while the boys were away at school, Doctor spent mornings at the hospital and afternoons at the downtown office. He invariably arrived in the morning with his first cigar about half smoked. After lunch, he always took a short nap on a couch in the basement dining room of the hospital, falling asleep with a lighted cigar in his mouth and snoring out of the other side. Everyone knew that, for their own sakes, they would best not interrupt that brief nap.

Doctor never took time for recreation in the strictest sense. He didn't play golf or have any such pursuit. His one habit for relaxation was to think of some reason to drive to Arnett or Higgins or Gage, get into his car and breeze away at a rapid clip. At any of these towns, he would visit with the banker or the county judge, chew the rag about politics and local matters, then drive back to Shattuck hospital at breakneck speed to make up for the time he had taken out.

One day in the winter of 1934, he and Dr. Davis had been to Arnett and were on their way north from the Ten Mile Store, coming down a hill about five miles south of Shattuck. It was a cold day and rain had frozen solid on the hillside. Just as Doctor started down the hill, someone was crossing, on foot, at the bottom. He put on his brakes and the big brown Buick went sliding and weaving down the slope. The pedestrian was now squarely in the middle and Doctor pulled left to avoid him and slammed into a shallow ditch. The heavy car did not turn over but rocked up on its right side wheels, throwing Doctor's chest against the steering wheel. He grunted and turned white.

"Doctor, are you hurt?" Dr. Davis cried.

"Just a little shaken up. I'm all right. Are you okay, John?"

"Plain scared is all. Let's get on home."

Doctor worked the rest of the day and went home in the evening for dinner as usual. Coming back for nightly rounds, he decided on a chest X-ray and found two broken ribs. He wore a jacket of adhesive tape the two following weeks to keep the pain bearable, but lost no work.

A little indulgence Doctor enjoyed was going to the bank when his pockets became stuffed with cash and checks. He enjoyed sitting back of the cage and visiting with J. H. C. Stuart, who took pride in handling the doctor's deposits personally. Mr. Stuart always seemed to doubt the adding machine, and after using it to total the amount, proceeded to add the figures in longhand. Another reason for Doctor's pleasure in this interlude was the opportunity to relax with another cigar.

Doctor was an official physician for the Santa Fe railway, and his travel was complimentary. When possible, he made his annual trip East and his northern jaunt to Mayo's in October or November, often accompanied by Mrs. Newman. At times, he attended Dr. John B. Murphy's clinics in Chicago, and spent a week at his old Ohio home. When he could get away, they spent a week in Texas in the spring.

His was a long-sighted view in regard to his patients. When he discovered that a person needed surgery, he did not try to push the idea upon him right away, unless it was an emergency. Following a consultation when major surgery was essential, the patient had left the room and Dr. Davis said, "Well, why doesn't he have his operation?"

"He's not quite ripe in his mind yet," Doctor replied. "We'll pluck him when he's ready in his own thinking."

Always philosophical, Doctor quite frequently injected dry humor into relations with his patients. Like the time when a doctor from Perryton, Texas sent a patient speedily to the Shattuck hospital and Dr. Newman. The trouble was gall bladder disease with stones, both in the bladder and the common duct.

"We can't delay," Doctor said earnestly, after examination. "This conditon calls for immediate surgery."

The husband of the patient waited a little, then said: "Well, Doctor, I think we're going to the Mayo clinic for this operation."

What the man didn't know was that Doctor had refused an offer from Mayo's to join their staff as a surgeon. But Doctor's face did not change expression as he remarked drily: "Well, they're good, too."

His esteemed partner for six years, Dr. John P. Davis said: "He never seemed to divide life into

... 131

good and bad. There was no dichotomy with him. Life was just what it was and there was no reason to get all stirred up about it. So it was that he never said 'This is good' or 'That's bad.' I presume his sincerety of this kept him from being a preacher, but it paid off in his inter-personal relationships. He could take a mediocre person and get the very finest type of work from him, not because he pushed that individual, but because he did not. He could get more work from an untrained girl than most doctors can from a registered nurse, because of their great desire to please him in return for his acceptance of them.

"Yet, his was not a passive nature; he had a strong will, but it was quiet and calmly philosophical and he was immune to adverse criticism."

Doctor's sore spot was any quackery in medicine, as pointed out in the case of the upstart and incompetent doctors who were his immediate superiors in the army. Somewhere around 1930, a doctor came to Shattuck and established private practice. Dr. Newman never thought in terms of competition; he thought there could never be too many good doctors. But before long, it was obvious that this person was a quack. His favorite diagnosis was diabetes and he had many people uselessly frightened in short order. From the Board of Medical Examiners, Doctor learned that the stranger was registered with them as being a graduate of the University of Lyons, France. That university wrote that he had never been a student there, and Doctor lost no time in getting the report to the Board and the quack out of town.

By 1935, all the boys were back in Shattuck, each a specialist, and practicing with his father in the hospital. Each year since, all of the doctor sons have spent some six weeks in New York, Baltimore, Chicago or at Mayo's taking further postgraduate courses in medicine, along the line of their specialties.

A memorandum of agreement, drawn up on January 12, 1937 made the four Newman doctors equal partners of the Shattuck Hospital. Dr. Fred L. Patterson was an additional surgeon, and on the staff were an anesthetist, a superintendent and ten nurses. The first year under this arrangement, ninty-seven per cent of the operative patients made a complete recovery.

Another expansion was imminent to adjoin the hospital, for examination rooms, laboratories and offices. The Newman Clinic was the result, built by the L. S. Fisher Construction company, of Woodward, with Albertis Montgomery the consulting engineer. The clinic was built with twenty rooms including a complete pharmacy and reception rooms.

The people of Shattuck and vicinity were in holiday spirit as the date approached for the formal opening and dedication of the clinic. Plans had been underway for weeks, and a great many citizens participated in both preparation and the event itself.

A committee composed of Mrs. George Suthers, chairman, with Mrs. Lester Wilson, Mrs. Herman Schultz, Mrs. E. J. Rader, Mrs. J. G. Richards, Mrs. J. J. Henry, Mrs. C. W. Nicholson and Mrs. M. M. Karn arranged with a young artist to paint the doctor's portrait for hanging in a place of honor. The dedication committee was Mr. and Mrs. J. G.

Richards, Lawrence Thomas, Eugene Tubb, Fred Teten and George Mason.

All business houses in town closed that day in August, 1937, and two thousand friends gathered in the high school auditorium. Banners throughout indicated seating sections: one for "babies" delivered by Doctor, another for pioneer friends from the days of old Grand, and other sections.

Doctor's heart was warmed and his eyes filled with tears to observe oldtimers O. H. and John Richards, Millard Word, O. E. Null, Hi Walck, Bill Boyd, G. A. Dean, A. A. Bennett, John McCullough, Anzley Ellis and many others.

This hand-lettered testimonial was created by oldtimer O. H. Richards at the time Doctor's portrait was presented by the persons to whom he attended at birth, painted by the student artist, Dord Fitz.

John Richards acted as master of ceremonies, the Shattuck high school band played, Dr. Wilmer E. Grindstaff gave the invocation, Mrs. M a r g a r e t Coleman-Wright directed singing by a chorus, O. H. Richards read a paper about Doctor's life and profession.

The mob of Doctor's "babies" sang, We're the Dr. Newman Babies" to the tune of "Hail, Hail the Gang's All Here," led by Marguerite McCartor. Honorable Charles Swindall, who had been attorney of old Day county and was later a Justice of the state supreme court gave an address filled with reminiscences. Mozelle Allison Jackson gave an original poem by Dr. Floyd Newman and Mary Josephine Reed sang a solo. Attorney Perry J. Morris, himself a pioneer gave the dedicatory address and the young artist, Dord Fitz was assisted by Doctor's granddaughter, JoAnn in making the presentation of the portrait.

Drs. Roy, Floyd and Haskell were hosts for open house at the new clinic and the people moved through the flower-filled rooms with all the pride of ownership, since Doctor had caused the townspeople to adopt this feeling.

Doctor came through the rooms, shaking hands, bringing some close friends with him. "I want your opinion about what kind of furniture to get for my office," he told them. "Most of the other furnishings are chrome and leather modern stuff, but secretly, I have a hankering for something more substantial looking."

They moved to the door of his office and went inside. Doctor stopped still in surprise and pleasure. There it was—fine, solid walnut furniture, the gift of his sons.

Friends coming to the dedication were not there so much to view the building of brick and steel, and to admire the scientific instruments but to honor Doctor, whom they all recognized as a great humanitarian.

That evening, a special program entertained nurses, technicians, doctors and dentists of a wide area. Dr. C. W. Tedrowe presided. Papers were read by Dr. Arthur H. Hertler, of Halstead, Kansas who was introduced by Dr. Bengerdis, of Beaver;

Dr. Everett S. Lain, Oklahoma City dermatologist, who was introduced by Dr. John L. Day, of Supply; Dr. M. O. Shivers, goiter specialist of Colorado Springs, who was introduced by Dr. C. R. Silverthorne. A pleasing factor to Doctor was the fact that Lain, Shivers and Silverthorne had all been classmates at the University of the South at Sewanee, Tennessee.

Nor did the hospital cease to grow and expand until it reached sixty-three rooms, completely air-conditioned. A new $150,000 addition was begun on July 30, 1947. A Ford Foundation grant in the spring of 1956 provided an entrance on the south, with a curving driveway and a canopied finish. Heretofore, it had been necessary for patients to enter the hospital through the maternity ward. With this improvement, the doorway opens into a vestibule and emergency room.

Frequently called the "Little Mayo of the West," the hospital and clinic became one of the most modern, best-equipped and efficiently staffed medical institutions in the southwest. At the clinic, besides the Newman doctors were added Dr. J. Mark Duncan, dentist; Mrs. Duncan, dental assistant; Garnet Hampton, laboratory technician; Bud Nicholson, pharmacist and Goldie Wilson Hunter, office nurse.

In 1949, the Newman Memorial Foundation was formed and the hospital was given to the city. The staff of physicians was made the managing board to operate as a non-profit making institution. In 1950, 29,229 patients registered at the clinic alone. They came from as far away as four hundred miles, hailing from southwest Kansas, southeast

Colorado, northeast New Mexico, northwest Texas and all of Oklahoma.

And so, the hospital of Doctor's dreams became a reality in his day.

The wheels, from hub to felloe, were filled with ice, resembling four large silver discs; icicles hung from the bed, and blobs of the stuff were stuck to the dashboard. The weary team standing in the shed displayed tails which were matted with ice halfway to the crupper, and pendant icicles hung from their manes.

CHAPTER X

Frozen Buggy Wheels

A great many people from all sections of the country have come forward with spoken and written recollections of Dr. O. C. Newman and his influence upon their lives. At the time of his induction into the Hall of Fame, Doctor was asked what period in his life held the fondest memories, to which he promptly replied: "Territorial days."

Remembering Doctor's choice, the author has selected from scores of contributions, both brief and lengthy, one offering to include almost in its entirety. O. Fant Word, of Hillsboro, Oregon has here expressed the admiration and respect held by so many thousands of people for the pioneer doctor. He speaks from personal experience of a long ago time most cherished in the memories of a great man.

> "I swear by Apollo, the physician, and Æsculpius, and health, and All-Heal— that, according to my ability and judgment, I will keep this Oath and this stipulation—and that by precept, lecture, and every mode of instruction, **I will impart a knowledge of the Art to my own sons**— and to disciples bound by stipulation and oath according to the law of medicine, but to none others. I will follow that system of regimen which, according to my ability

and judgment, I consider for the benefit of my patients, and abstain from whatever is deleterious and mischievous. I will give no deadly medicine to anyone if asked, nor suggest any such counsel. With purity and with holiness I will pass my life and practice my Art.

Into whatever houses I enter, I will go into them for the benefit of the sick, and will abstain from every voluntary act of mischief and corruption. Whatever, in connection with my professional practice or not, I see or hear, in the life of man, which ought not to be spoken abroad, I will not divulge, as reckoning that all such should be kept secret. While I continue to keep this Oath unviolated, may it be granted to me to enjoy life, and the practice of the Art, **respected by all men, in all times!** But should I trespass and violate this Oath, may the reverse be my lot." (Author's note: Above phrases from the Hippocratic Oath which are seen in bold face apply significantly and literally to the life and profession of Dr. Newman.)

The above lines are excerpts from the Oath of Hippocrates, who is sometimes called the "Father of Medicine." He laid down this meticulous code of moral and professional ethics over four hundred years before the Christian era. Half a thousand years later, Galen, another great pioneer in the science of medicine, referred to him as "the legislator of medicine." In no important particular has the code been altered in the centuries that followed.

It is my intent to convey here a fleeting glimpse

of a man who, like unto Luke, was another "beloved physician." How well this man's life and works were embraced by the Hippocratic Oath, the reader may judge from the testimony of those whose lives and orbits touched his, and who were benefitted in body and spirit by that association.

From the folio of more than fifty years ago, I would like to place here a small vignette of a winter morning. The year was 1904, the setting, the little frontier town of Grand, Day county, Oklahoma Territory, on the banks of the South Canadian river.

I was six years old and had started to school that fall, riding horseback from our ranch home three miles upriver. As severe cold moved in, my parents arranged for me to stay with the young doctor and his wife for better access to school. In this manner, I first made the acquaintance of Dr. Oscar C. Newman, his wife Della, and their eldest son, Roy, who was not far from the "toddler" stage. They lived in a small two-room house which had an open-front shed at the back for the doctor's team.

On this particular morning, it was bitterly cold. I went outside and "took a look at the weather." The buggy stood near the shed, and I noted that it looked unfamiliar, being almost sheathed in ice. The wheels, from hub to felloe, were filled with ice, resembling four large silver discs; icicles hung from the bed, and blobs of the stuff were stuck to the dashboard. The weary team standing in the shed displayed tails which were matted with ice halfway to the crupper, and pendant icicles hung from their manes. Being pretty well chilled myself by now, I hurried into the house and announced my observations to Mrs. Newman, asking her, in effect "How come?" She "shushed" me—the doctor was sleeping—then explained that Doctor had been across the river and the team and buggy had broken through the ice, coming home.

A small thing, you may say. Possibly so. But to me then, and now, it was impressive. It was not an uncommon experience for men who dared that treacherous stream to have similar or worse things happen to them. Still, the mental quirk was then imprinted on a child's mind, and in later years this image would recur at any contemplation upon the doctor's personality. It became a symbol, and that symbol seems to encompass his indomitable will, his resolution to answer the call of distressed and suffering humanity, his selfless dedication to his high calling—the profession of medicine.

The rest of that winter was pretty much made up of repeat performances. I rarely saw him, save when he was sleeping, or rousing up to answer another urgent summons, or coming home, wan and weary, his eyes reddened from lack of sleep. Still, he had time for a kindly word to me, now and then.

How many, many miles he drove in those beginning years! Roads were scarcely more than two ruts or in many instances, just a trace. In the arctic cold of winter and the searing heat of summer, he worked through all the seasons. If snow or flood or the terrain were too rugged for the buggy, he rode horseback. For many of these calls, he was not paid, as a considerable number of his homesteader patients were wretchedly poor in everything but hopes. The "claims" were located over a lot of country, on or near one of the numerous tributary creeks which wound down to the river. The names of these watercourses stir nostalgic memories— Little Turkey, Mosquito Creek, Red Bluff, Little Robe, Commission, Hackberry, Packsaddle, and more. The doctor knew them all, and the people who had bet Uncle Sam ten dollars that they could "prove up" a title to the homestead and not starve to death ere three years were up! Some went the distance, but some had to welch the bet, and pull out.

If this recording has presented their lives in a grim light, let it be hastily added that the picture is incomplete. Hardships were endured, yes, but there were compensations to offset them.

How strange and different must have been his new surroundings, when this stripling medical student, an alien in a strange land, came from the staid Ohio valley in 1900! Much of this area was still virgin prairie, unscarred by the plow. He saw rolling grasslands where prairie chicken abounded. The bobwhite sent his liquid call over dew-drenched meadows in the mornings, and the white, moon-magic summer nights were filled by the mockingbird's song.

It can be assumed that his senses thrilled at being a part of the settlement of a new land, the chance to dare the untried, to savor the excitement and share the soaring dreams of these venturesome ones who came to claim this part of the diminishing frontier. His roots sank deep in this, his adopted land, and when he cast his lot with the other settlers, it was for keeps!

Years later, when this little town had vanished, some of the former residents set up an annual date for a reunion of old Day county residents. They were scattered far and wide, but a surprisingly large number of them managed to attend these yearly picnics. Dr. O. C. Newman allowed himself few personal indulgences, but this was one, and he seldom missed attending.

Many stories, some probably apocryphal, were clustered about this busy young man. Still single and not yet established in medical practice, he plied various jobs to make expenses. There was one relating to a time when he was a deputy county clerk. One day when all of the regular officials were absent, there came a couple who desired a marriage license. Deputy Newman obliged, and made out application and license. The couple inquired about a minister or official who could marry them. No such person being available at the moment, they put the matter up to him, with the plausible argument that if he could legally make up the record, it followed that he could also perform the marriage. This sounded reasonable enough, so after some searching in the Judge's desk, O. C. found the text of the judicial ceremony, procured witnesses and proceeded with the marriage. The couple paid the fees and departed, across the river, for parts unknown.

When informed that this affair was without legal sanction, he made a strenuous effort to locate the people, without success. It was many years later when he heard of them. They were living in another state and had raised a large family of children. His chuckled comment: "Well, it must have been a binding contract—it seemed to hold together all right."

144 . . .

Another yarn concerned an incident which occurred at a time when his finances were at low ebb. Despite his part time jobs, he had fallen far behind with his board bill, and his clothes were wearing out. He went into the general store one day to make some small purchase, and as he turned to leave, the storekeeper, a blunt, laconic gent whose name was Sam Cupp, noticed that the seat of his pants had worn through. Sam said, "Doc, go over to that table and get you some pants."

The doctor, with some diffidence, replied: "Mr. Cupp, I don't have the money to pay you."

Sam shouted back, "Who said anything about pay? I said 'go git them pants!'" The doctor obeyed.

Sometimes he filled in as barkeeper in the town's saloon. In this capacity, he was strictly the dispenser; so far as is known, he was a teetotaller. It was an experience which he rather liked to recall. I think it tickled his fancy to reflect that he had once been, ever so briefly, a bartender! The experience was doubtless beneficial, for this man was deeply a student of psychology, and he studied it "on the hoof." He acquired an uncanny amount of knowledge about people; how their minds worked, what made them tick.

My parents, Millard and Bessie Word, had a sort of proprietary interest in the young doctor. They had been the earliest settlers in this part of the Territory. They had watched his early struggles and had most fervently wanted him to stay on and establish a practice. And they were inordinately proud that he did surmount the obstacles and attain to the great success which he accomplished.

My mother once went to see a neighbor lady who was quite ill. Several other women were there, some of whom felt that they were qualified to undertake treatment. Dr. Newman had been summoned, and as he made examination, he was bombarded with suggestions from the ladies who knew various nostrums, poultices and remedies which would infallibly cure.

My mother listened with mounting annoyance. Finally, she drew the doctor aside and gave vent to her indignation. She said, "Doctor, I want you to tell these people that you are the physician here, and that you will prescribe the treatment!"

He remained quite unperturbed, was in fact, deeply amused. He chuckled and replied, "Well now, Mrs. Word, none of those 'treatments' would really hurt her any. They might even do some good if the patient felt they would help."

My mother felt rather chastened, but was still fuming a little when she got home. "Those old women! Trying to tell our doctor how to treat his patient." This happened many years before the public prints began to discuss the medical profession's recognition of the importance of mental therapeutics. Dr. O. C. probably knew this when he started to practice.

The phase I have attempted to set down here deals mainly with Dr. Newman's Day county residence, as that was the beginning of his distinguished career. A rough beginning, a hard-won experience which set the pattern for his life's work.

Like Sir William Osler, whom he greatly admired, Dr. Newman was not only a very outstanding physician and surgeon, he was equally a great humanitarian. He received many honors, in and outside his professional field, all well deserved. But I think the greatest tribute he received was not a bronze tablet, a parchment scroll, or engraved certificate. It was an enshrined place in the hearts of the hundreds of people whom he has served. There were folk to whom he had come in dark hours, when body and mind were sick and despair was spreading its awful desolation. His healing magic had dispelled the pain and suffering, his fine surgeon's mind had guided dexterous fingers to remove some harbinger of death from tortured tissues, and his calm, unruffled voice had restored hope when hope had failed. He knew this, of course, though he did not speak of it. There was no trace of arrogance in his make up.

When you walk and talk with a fellow man, you are too close, and his presence too warmly human and familiar to gauge his full stature. Only when his characteristics and abilities are viewed from some distance of time and place can one gain the perspective necessary to evalute the essence of greatness. It is not given to everyone to have known intimately a truly great man. That privilege was mine, and for the privilege, I shall be always grateful.

CHAPTER XI

DOCTOR YOU INSPIRED US

(Author's note: The good people across the nation who knew Dr. O. C. Newman have been generous in their response to our request for personal experiences and incidents relating to the colorful life of the pioneer physician. We are indebted to these friends and former patients, without whom this biography could not have been written. Many responses came in the form of a written tribute, some of which are included here, in whole or in part.)

MY DOCTOR

Kind angels, when you meet him there, let one
Bright wing droop helplessly, as if in need.
Or dim, if but a little while the sun
Of your perfection; for his healing plead.
And down the golden streets of those sweet lands,
Point out some heavenly homes; and promise him
That some of these will seek restoring hands
And kindly cheer, as did the sons of men.
For if he cannot help and come at call,
It will not heaven be to this brave soul,
Whose life was spent a ministry to all
But self: love of humanity his dole.
Let him believe, until he learns Your way,
That need of him will bless each busy day.

                              Daisy Thorne Gilbert

In the year 1916, in an isolated country home, Dr. Newman performed what I choose to call a miracle. A girl of nine had been given up by another doctor, following thirteen convulsions. Dr. Newman prepared for immediate operation, chloroforming the child and opening veins in her arm and her ankle. A pint or more of black blood was removed, and then, by some ingenious, home method, he forced sterilized, salty water in her veins. A few weeks later, the patient had completely recovered from uremic poisoning.

Austa Parker Gilson

> I saw him in a dim light,
>   at the birth of our son.
> I saw him in a bright light,
>   at the dedication of his clinic.
> I saw him in the candlelight,
>   as he was inducted into the Hall of Fame.
> I saw him in a heavenly light,
>   the night he joined his church.
> I saw him in a kindly light,
>   in his home and mine.
> I saw him in the twilight,
>   as he was laid to rest.
> "Well done, thy good and faithful servant."
>
> Mozelle Allison Jackson

My husband, the late J. G. Richards enjoyed with Dr. Newman a Damon and Phintias-like friendship. He came across the country from Ohio, where his friend added a year to his waning heart, though it apparently aroused professional jealousy in the Ohio physician who told my husband to "go on back to his little tin god in Oklahoma."

I remember vividly an incident when Dr. and Mrs. Newman were our hosts at a dinner in Oklahoma City. When my order of jumbo frog legs was placed before me, Doctor remarked that they reminded him of a "premature" which he had recently delivered. The expression on my face and my rapidly failing appetite was Doctor's reward.

Audrey Richards

During the second World War, I tried to keep the doctor in cigars. One day, I went up to the hospital with what I could hold in my hand. Doctor was standing outside a back door smoking a little short pipe. I reached around and held that handful of cigars in front of him. Doctor just tossed that pipe out in the yard, and without looking around, took the cigars and said, "Well, bless your heart."

John Barcafer

Money was no object with Dr. Newman. When I was sixteen, it became necessary for me to have my appendix removed. My father had been injured a few months before, and since he had a family of six children, we were a little short of money. Later, when my father went to pay our hospital bill, Dr. Newman had no record of it at all. We paid the bill, but if we had been dishonest or careless, we could have kept the $125 and probably he would never have remembered it.

Mrs. J. R. Reed

There are many things which I remember about my Uncle Oscar, but that which impressed me most deeply was the following. He came after me to go with him on his motorcycle to call on a patient living in the country. I was dressed up in my best and as proud as a little girl can be when her favorite uncle is taking her on an important trip.

He lifted me to the rear seat of the motorcycle and in doing so, he said, "Now, this little gadget here is hot. Put your knee on it." I did just that and he took me into the house and dressed the burn, then we started out again.

I shall never forget the concerned expression on his face when he told me: "Now, Murl, let that be a lesson to you not to do everything that just anybody tells you to do."

Murl Travis
(daughter of Joseph (Dock) Smith)

Perhaps the closest comradeship known to man is that between soldiers on the field of battle. I like to think of the bond of friendship between Dr. O. C. and your's truly as being that kind of comradeship. Being a public figure, he has many times been the subject of a story in my newspaper. But our comradeship was not confined to interviews; I have enjoyed many little chats with him, and drawn inspiration from his homely philosophy.

In 1951, while he was undergoing treatment at Mayo's, I composed a bit of verse to him and published it in the paper, expressing the thought above. And I ended it sincerely, with these lines:

So, Dr. and Mrs., this poem must end,
Though its writing was fun, and a cinch;
We at NWO wish you return to health,
And to Shattuck, the best town per inch.

C. C. Colbert, Editor
The Northwest Oklahoman

My acquaintance with him dates back some fifty years, when Doctor was at Grand and I at Cheyenne. Through the years, our practice overlapped and we have spent many earnest consultations together. He was strictly ethical, not only in his dealings with patients, but with other physicians. Can one say more?

C. W. Tedrowe, M.D.

Dr. Newman served with great distinction and fidelity. He was a master at the art of helping people; the ministry of his radiant personality began the healing even before treatment or medication.

Rev. Robert R. Chambers

I taught in the Shattuck schools from 1924 to 1927, living that last year in the home of Dr. and Mrs. Newman while the boys were all away at college. It took some persuasion on my part to gain admission, but we were soon all one family. To this struggling school teacher, the spacious, beautifully furnished home, together with the congenial atmosphere was an appreciated haven at the close of a day in the classroom. During this year, friendships were formed which have been treasured through the years. I noticed particularly that no matter how often the telephone rang, or at what hour of the night, there was never a word of complaint from Mrs. Newman.

After a full life of service, we can say of him in the words of Paul Dunbar:

"When all is done, say not my day is o'er,
And that through night I see a dimmer shore;
Say rather that my morn has just begun;
I greet the dawn and not a setting sun,
When all is done."

Josephine Thomas

In 1925, my son Walter had a ruptured appendix operation, followed by more serious surgery two weeks later, and a third operation fifty days later. I had paid $125 and while staying to be close to

. . . 153

my son, I had no place to room. The Newmans were building their new house and Doctor told me: "You go down to the place and Roy will give you a job and Mrs. Newman will give you something to eat."

So I helped Roy to tear down some old buildings and worked on the new one while the good woman fed me like one of the family.

The following year, I took Walter back for a check-up and Goldie said, "Doctor, that man who has owed you $40 for so long came and paid up." Dr. Newman told her quickly: "Goldie, give the man back his money. He needs it more than we do."

George Gantz

I had the honor of sitting between General Keys and the Ambassador from Mexico the night Doctor's portrait was placed in the state Hall of Fame. I was also the main speaker on other occasions when he was honored. As his pastor, I received more high honors than in the other twenty years I have been a minister.

Rev. C. Chalon Meadows

My brother-in-law, Robert Rang, a young boy, was stricken ill and suffering much pain. Other doctors treated him with narcotics for thirty or forty days, then gave him up. I was sent to notify relatives, and called on Dr. Newman to come. He arrived about sundown, asked questions, made examination, then sat in a deep study for about two hours.

Finally, he said he was fully confident the disease was trichinosis and set about mixing his

154 . . .

own medicine. After the boy recovered, he revealed that he had been in the habit of eating raw, cured ham, though he had no way of knowing that raw pork carries the worms which cause this disease.

Ray C. Ingle

In speaking of Dr. Newman, I will use his favorite name for me, and will refer to him by that name which he coveted most. I am "the little Indian preacher;" he is "the country doctor."

I met him on my first pastoral call to the patients at the Newman hospital. We talked of many things that day. He was more like a historian getting the story of my life; he was fascinated by the fact that an Indian had become a preacher. He was a "searcher for the truth," a "seeker after God."

Though a compassionate man, working side by side with God in his calling, he had not actually confessed faith in Jesus Christ and united with the church until my ministry with him, and it was a prime experience in my life to baptize him.

During his last conscious days, I prayed at his bedside. I heard his whispered amen, then he said, "It was a good prayer, little Indian. It was a good prayer. Everything's all right now, little Preacher." A few days later, Dr. Newman had "gone home."

And so, Doctor's long search for God came to an end. The little Indian preacher and the white country doctor together found Jesus, and in finding Jesus, the country doctor found God.

Rev. Lewis M. Hancock

Dr. O. C. seemed to like me and my work. Never would he let another technician take a blood count if I was on duty. The only way we could tell when he was below par, himself, was by the slowness of his work. The first time he failed to come to the hospital, Dr. Roy had me go out to his home for a CBC.

Doctor declared, "If I had wanted this, I would have ordered it myself," but he allowed me to proceed, one of those truly rare times when he was the patient.

Norma E. Kolander, M.T.

I met him first when I was a young woman with three small children. Physically, I had gone as far as I could go, and mentally, I was in tears. It isn't easy for a mother of small children to be told by other doctors that she has about one chance in a hundred of coming back to them after surgery. I wish I had adequate words to say how his calm assurance relieved my fears! I went home with a lighter heart, and the Great Physician gave me victory through the dedicated hands of Dr. Newman.

No task was too difficult, no work too lowly for him. From fording the raging Canadian in the early days and operating on a little boy in the home, to windlassing an elevator in the old hospital with his own hands, he did all with skill and patience.

Stella Isenhower Flewelling

There is one thing I think Doctor would like for the reader to know. After making his profession of faith and while waiting for baptism, he wondered if the church, or any average auditorium would be large enough to hold all the people he had delivered into the world, and expressed the wish that they could all witness his baptism.

Opal Booth Karn, R.N.

All through this life he walked with steady tread,
And where he walked, the pattern of life's play
Was full and warm with sympathy that led
The grievous heart to meet another day.
And when his magic hands out-distanced death,
A light, exultant, burned in grateful eyes.
His heart poured warmth and courage, and each breath
Spoke miracles that stilled hurt-human cries!
His simple faith, his love for all mankind
Was beautiful to see. Assurance, calm,
A gentle strength to ease the worried mind
Was like the balm of Gilead. A balm
Of God's own servitude and gentleness
For dedicated hands that heal and bless!

Stella Isenhower Flewelling

If Dr. O. C. were alive today and was told that a book was being written on his life and how it affected others, he would smile gratefully and say, "Is that right?" then walk away to minister to his patients.

Naomi Dalrymple Meier

My acquaintance with Dr. Newman began when Ellis county was placed in my district in 1933. While holding court in Ellis county, I rarely had a court term but that Dr. Newman was a witness for the state or defendant in criminal cases. We had an arrangement with Dr. Newman that when he was needed, he would be called by phone and he always came without fail; he did not require a subpoena. In most cases, his testimony was the deciding factor in the case, as the jurors had all confidence in the evidence he gave, since they knew he could not be influenced by anyone. Dr. Newman was my per-

sonal physician from the time I met him until
his death.

Judge F. Hiner Dale

If I had an armful of glory—
A carved shaft of granite to name,
And I had the gift of an artist
Whose canvasses whispered of fame,
I'd splash you a picturesque story
That would fill, full, a fine marble hall,
And its character study of honor
Would shine, truly shine, wall to wall.
And I'd lay my armful of glory,
As a tribute of honor and pride,
At the feet of this country doctor
And the helpmate who stood by his side.
And the name that I'd carve on the granite
Would whisper new hope through the years;
A silent reminder, a symbol
Of hope versus heartache and tears!

Stella Isenhower Flewelling

Doctor Newman enabled me to continue my
college education when all looked hopeless. I did
not ask for help, but somehow, he sensed my
plight, for the same day I was about to leave
Lubbock and come home, I received in the mail
his check for a hundred dollars and a brief letter
telling me that success is a matter of determination
and constant application. So I unpacked and have
ever since tried to follow his advice.

After I received my degree, I taught Vocation-
al Agriculture a term before I came home to pay
what I owed him. He chuckled and asked, "Leo,
did I give you any money to go to school?"

Before my marriage, he called me into his
office to approve my choice in a mate. Dr. Newman
was an applied student of psychology.

158 . . .

In 1947, we moved to Doctor's farm in Follett, Texas where we now reside. During the remaining years of his life, he constantly reminded me: "Could I help you in some way? If you are short on operating expenses, I'll be glad to help."

After my very first crop here, I asked him if he wished to sell his own wheat. He replied: "No, you sell mine. If you make a profit, so will I. Otherwise, I'll take my loss along with you. You aren't doing this just for your health."

When he came out to the farm, he never failed to get out of the car and go directly to the windmill for a fresh drink of water, and remark: "I believe this is the best water in the world."

Leo Meier

After moving away from Shattuck in 1917, I returned there annually for thirty-three years, always paying a visit to my old friend. He repaid my visit yearly when he came to Mayo's in Rochester, just ninety miles from my home in Minneapolis.

Dr. Newman always thought first of others. He worshipped his family and always dreamed of the boys becoming doctors and practicing with him in Shattuck. When I saw him each year, he would review the progress and relate his plans.

Dr. and Mrs. Newman visited with us in 1940, when we all went to a famous Smorgasbord at the Hotel St. Paul where you could eat all you wanted for seventy-five cents. That was Doctor's first experience with smorgasbord, and he ate seven different kinds of pastries and desserts.

They visited us another year, where Doctor saw his first television program while Mrs. Newman and my wife were shopping for her attendance at his installation dinner in Oklahoma City as the Outstanding Citizen of Oklahoma. His every thought was of his wife, and he kept waiting for the time when they were to meet us. I remember how proud he was of the dress, with purse and gloves to match that she had bought to wear at that special event.

James M. Tuthill

Recalling the life and career of Dr. O. C. Newman recalls the Antelope Hills and the little town, old Grand, which he greatly loved. There was the general store, the postoffice, the horse-drawn mail wagon swaggering a typical pioneer spirit. And the mighty South Canadian! The sand bars of the big river sprawled far and wide, flowing and blowing or just sleeping, only to rise again, defying all efforts of man since the beginning of time.

Today the big river seems to be working on the outer rim of the great horseshoe bend, pushing it back and away from the hills, perhaps leaving them to the will of time and eternity. Or leaving them to appease the angry gods of mad red water!

It was only recently that I went down again to the Antelope Hills. There I lingered. I roamed over those hills and I viewed once more with deep interest the great river. I thought back to the South Canadian flood of 1908 when thousands of acres of fine land were swept away. I could envision the plight of those settlers when their humble homes and meager belongings were carried away by the merciless flood. I could see there, destitution, sickness and death.

And then I could see a stalwart young doctor, right among the hard-hit settlers. I could see him steering his horse to avoid the treacherous quick-sand to where there was urgent need for him. I could see the outlaw cayuse buck him over its head into the boiling river, with his medicine kit carried swiftly downstream.

There again was Doctor climbing in and out of a stranded covered wagon to allay the wracked and delirious brain of a child suffering from high fever, at a time when care was crude, and housing a dream of the future.

In memory today I still see this once stalwart bronc-busting doctor who staked a chance far out in the sage and sand dunes, and who as time passed could spin the crank of a Model T until it was glad to go. It is not because of hoarded wealth or gaudy glamor, but because he hung onto the wil-

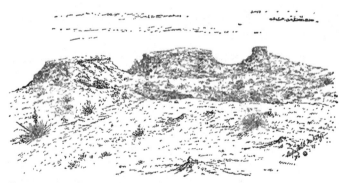

"It was only recently that I went down again to the Antelope Hills, and there, I lingered, roaming over them."

lows and toughed it out that he was rightly selected and proclaimed a worthy member of Oklahoma Hall of Fame.

Solon Porter
(author of Ragged Roads)

One morning in the early 1920's Dr. O. C. Newman called me into his office on Main street. "Frank," he said, "I have some lots which have grown up in weeds. I want those lots cleared, but I don't want the weeds chopped down; I want them pulled up by the roots. Go over and look at them and tell me what you think it's worth to pull them."

I surveyed the jungle of chest high weeds, pulled a small section and estimated that I could pull them in two days. Therefore, I proposed to pull the weeds for five dollars. No doubt Dr. Newman realized that my youthful judgment was optimistic, but with a twinkle in his eye, he said, "When can you begin?" My reply was translated into immediate and aggressive action, which began to wane with the withering assault of the summer sun which baked the earth and made the work more and more difficult.

One week later, after having spent a considerable part of the anticipated profits on gloves and liniment, a weary lad reported to the doctor that the job was finished. He inspected the work, thanked me for a good job and handed me a five-dollar bill.

A few years later, I decided to have a tonsillectomy before leaving for college. Upon asking for my statement, Dr. Newman told me the amount it would be, but suggested that I wait until the following summer to pay. When summer came and I went to his office to pay my bill, his nurse, Goldie, presented me a bill which was for half the original figure. When I reminded her that the amount was less than I had understood, she replied that Dr. Newman had instructed her to reduce it.

Whether the doctor was reflecting on a boy who sadly miscalculated and lived up to his bargain, or whether this was his way of helping a young ministerial student obtain an education, I will never know, but certainly this act characterized the spirit of a man who always gave to others more than he expected of them.

Frank W. Patterson

(Author's note: Frank W. Patterson, of El Paso, Texas received his Doctor's degree in May, 1957, from a seminary in Kansas City. He is head of the Spanish translation publishing house of the Southern Baptist Convention. He and his wife, Pauline Gilliland, attended seminary in Fort Worth and he graduated from Oklahoma Baptist University in Shawnee, Oklahoma. Patterson's wife is a staff writer of Sunday School lessons.)

The Mayo Clinic, of Rochester, Minnesota had made Dr. O. C. Newman a tempting offer to join their staff. Naturally, the townspeople were quite uneasy at the prospect of losing their beloved physician. Dr. Newman's simple reply in words to this effect, gladdened the hearts of all in the Shattuck community: "All that I have, I have received from the people of this area; all that I am, I expect to give to the people of this area." It was not just superior skill as a surgeon which endeared Dr.

Newman to people far and near, but his spirit of compassionate self-dedication.

Frank W. Patterson

When people reminisce about Dr. Newman, I often think of what the husband of one of my cousins said about him. I told my relatives at Piedmont, Oklahoma that Roy Newman, of Shattuck, and I were soon to be married. A short time after that, my cousin made several week long quail hunting trips to northwest Oklahoma. He spent the nights at a Shattuck hotel, and during the day, he would hunt, down near the river. Without telling anyone that his cousin was engaged to Dr. Newman's son, he began listening and asking some questions, to learn what he could about the Newmans, as he was interested in finding out what kind of family "Jennie" (as he called me) was marrying into. After several hunting trips he told me, "I never found a man that didn't like Dr. Newman. Everyone that mentioned him had something good to say of him."

After being Dr. Newman's daughter-in-law for a number of years I can see why everyone liked him. Besides being the best doctor, I thought so at any rate, he was the kindest and most understanding father-in-law anyone could have.

Virginia Newman
(wife of Dr. Roy E. Newman)

Doctor Newman never longed for the toga of fame, yet it fell gently upon his shoulders and he wore it with quiet poise and dignity. He had a long record of patient and efficient service to the sick and needy. No wonder he was able to count his friends by the thousands.

Hardship and poverty of the early days would have been a chain around the character of a lesser man. Yet he bore it in a way that actually made others proud of their poverty and suffering. There was a time when the blowing soil of the Dust Bowl threatened to drive him from the land that he loved, yet he lived to see one of the fairest flowers of medical service blooming from this very soil.

With this full story of Dr. Newman's life written in a book, many will read it with great profit. Yet, let us ever remember that we can trace the course and influence of his life more readily in the hearts of the people he touched than we can in the ink of his biographer.

Wilmer E. Grindstaff, D.D.

AN ACROSTIC BASED ON THE NAME OF O. C. NEWMAN

O-OURS, OTHERS. One explanation of our great love for him was that he had the unique ability to make all of us know that he was our's in a peculiar way. His life was lived in unselfish devotion to the welfare of others and with little concern for his own.

C - CHRISTIAN CITIZEN, CHRIST - LIKE CHARACTER. In the roster of northwest Oklahoma citizens, the name of Newman leads the rest. His profession of faith was not the act of an aging and frightened man, but that of a man who had reached the peak of his wisdom and come to the conclusion that Christ was all. This was the crowning act of a great intellect.

N-NOBLE NAME. The name of Newman is the most respected and honored in this community.

It is a synonym of respectability, service and quiet dignity. To mention it is to evoke warm words of praise.

E-EARNEST, ENTHUSIASTIC. He met the suffering of others with becoming earnestness, treating each seriously. To this virtue, he added an enthusiasm for living. He was enthusiatic about setting human feet on the road to recovery. He was an enthusiastic supporter of every good cause, most of all for the cause of the Kingdom.

W-WORSHIPFUL WORKER. Surgery was to him an act of worship. He learned long ago that one can only serve God by serving mankind.

M-MAN AMONG MEN. The honors that came as a Doctor of Medicine did not overshadow the fact of his manhood. In any gathering of men, he was seated at the head of the table.

A-ACHIEVEMENTS. His achievements were acclaimed far and wide. For the occasion of paying to him our last respects, there were messengers and messages from all walks of life, from the governor of the state to the humblest townsman. He did not become great when he was inducted into the Hall of Fame; that act was merely the outward recognition of his greatness.

N-NEAR WHEN NEEDED. "He was always near when needed." This characterizes the man who seldom took a vacation and was to be counted upon in any distress. He was not unduly impressed by his fame, and entirely too busy to enjoy his prosperity.

Wilmer E. Grindstaff
Assistant Executive Secretary
Baptist General Convention
of Oklahoma

Thank you, God, for an uncommon man! He had the faith to follow his strengthening trust in Thee. Specializing in helpfulness, Dr. Newman stored up no animosities and nursed no grudges.

An uncommon man, he could pierce the farce of littleness and escape the tensions that beset men of weak will. He knew the power to condemn belonged to Thee alone, therefore his heart betrayed no resentment housed within. Perhaps that is why you heard his plea for pardon. He learned to love Your Son who was also an Uncommon Man, and a Great Physician.

Speak to him, Lord, and let him know that his friends look forward to further fellowship with this uncommon man. Amen.

Dr. Wilmer E. Grindstaff

CHAPTER XII

ONE MAN'S SONS

The first thing I remember of ever hearing, as to the feeling my dad had toward his own children, is a story my mother has told to me in the past. It was back in the early days in old Day county in the Oklahoma Territory. Annually, the settlers met at Grand, which was the county seat and our home, for a picnic. Dad would carry me around the picnic grounds and k e e p feeding me ice cream until I could eat no more. Then, knowing in advance that it was coming, he would treat me for the colic all night.

Roy E. Newman, M.D.

Then, as I reached school age, it became advisable to get rid of the Buster Brown hair-do I was wearing. One day, Mother sent me to town alone and asked Dad to have my hair cut. No one would have thought of Dad as being sentimental, but before he took me to the barber shop, he stopped at Henry Rothenburger's studio and had my picture made. There I was, barefooted, and in a little everyday pair of straight pants, probably hand made by my mother, and blouse and Buster Brown hair-do. Well, for many years, every time I would visit any of our relatives, they would bring out their copy of this picture.

Later, I was probably nine or ten years of age, another doctor moved to Shattuck. I had overheard, as children will, some uncomplimentary things this doctor had been saying about my dad, and naturally, it hurt me no end. One day, I approached Dad with the tales and saw, for the first time, how big he really was.

"Roy," he said gently. "Don't let things like that worry you, ever. If competition is good and clean, learn to work with them. But, if the competition is not what it should be and they start telling things that are not true about you, then just you sit tight, and keep your mouth closed and your eyes and ears open. They will move shortly." In this case, that is just what happened.

And that was the philosophy he practiced throughout his life. He was a lover and respecter of his fellow man. He would never stand and listen to idle gossip, regardless of the standing in the community held by the speaker or the person being slandered.

Another instance which indicates the feeling Dad had toward his fellow man occurred after I was practicing medicine with him and my younger brothers. We had a call from a lawyer who made adjustments for our liability insurance carriers. I was the one who talked to him. He stated that a certain family was taking steps to sue us for malpractice due to the death of the head of the family.

170 . . .

"Do you feel," the lawyer asked at the outset, "the same as your father in respect to these suits?"

I said, "How is that?"

"Dr. O. C. said that he is confident no jury in Ellis county would find him guilty of malpractice in any suit."

"No," I declared. "I don't have quite that much faith in people anywhere."

Well, the suit did not develop, but this incident shows the faith Dad had in his people.

My father was one of the greatest students and teachers I have ever known, and I say this humbly. I was still a pre-medical student and home for a few days vacation. I had been associating with a bunch of pharmacy students who were studying for the State Board. I hadn't taken any courses which contained dosage or prescription of drugs, but at one of these "bull sessions" I absorbed memory of the dosage for tincture of digitalis.

While at home, I was on call with Dad up in the northern part of the county. I thought that he had been out of school for so long that he wouldn't remember the U.S.P. dosage which I had carefully memorized, so I proceeded to catch him. "Do you know the dosage of tincture of digitalis?" I put the question to him.

"Well," he said, "The U.S.P. dose is ten to twelve minims (drops) but I give it in teaspoonsful. You know, Son, we don't give medicine for the fun of it, but for the effect on the patient." At that time, I didn't know the importance of this particular drug in the treatment of heart diseases, but I have

. . . 171

since learned to respect it as one of our most vital drugs.

When I was a junior in medical school, Dad and I were again discussing the practice of medicine. Of course, it didn't take him long to see how little I knew of the practical side of the profession. In our conversation, Dad said, "I'll teach you boys more about real practice during the first year we work together than you'll learn in your years of medical school." And believe me, he did.

Another instance of his teaching ability was told me by a friend of Dad's who had studied with him on postoperative work. It was in Chicago and the instructor in operative surgery was called out of town. Dad had studied this course several times, but felt it paid to repeat it each year, if possible. While the instructor was out of town for a couple of days, he asked Dad to take his place. The doctor who told me this said that the whole class regretted to see the return of the regular instructor, though he was an excellent teacher of operative surgery, for they had gotten more from Dad's lectures and demonstrations.

A rare trait in my father was his acceptance of our mistakes in diagnosis and treatment without abuse or belittlement. Yet, we seldom made the same mistake twice, for through his patient reasoning with us, we corrected our procedures. He taught us carefully that where there is a cause, there is effect, and vice versa. This same treatment was applied to other doctors who came with patients for consultation. He would never make the other doctor feel he had been lectured, but would give him the feeling that Dad had merely helped him recall something that had slipped his mind. Neither was the patient made to think that his home physician was inferior in any way; usually, they got the impression that they were seeing Dr. Newman because he had more facilities with which to work, thereby enabling a more complete examination and diagnosis. He would never ask these patients to return to **him**, but to keep in contact with his home physician, through whom he could be reached if advisable.

Dad's teaching and philosophy is pretty well brought out in a quotation on a little wooden plaque which I saw hanging over the writing desk of that grand lady, Mrs. Effie Stuart. It states: "It isn't what you know, but what you learn after you know it all, that counts."

Dr. Roy E. Newman

An Ohio farm is the back-
    ground,
Where a family of New-
    man's dwelled.
They were known as a fam-
    ily of plenty,
Where gladness and happi-
    ness swelled.
In this little Ohio family,
That I am relating about:
Ten children made up a true
    gladness,
Which must have b e e n
    their's without doubt.

F. S. Newman, M.D.

One son was not a good worker,
Especially at labor, they said.
No work at cement and mortar,
For he was a student instead.

This son, whose name was Oscar
Went to college to read and to learn;
He went for some years as a worker
And much midnight oil did he burn.

After four long years of college,
He finished the medical course;
He left for the West to practice,
To live from only this source.
At first in that unbroken country,
Where lacking and scarce was gold,
And all of the people were needy,
His living was scant, we are told.

Four years of this hard, rough living,
Four years of this little and lack;
Not always at ease when eating,
And little the clothes on his back.
But when those four years were over,
He met with his first love true.
It was Miss Della Smith that he honored,
Who was faithful as blue is blue.

Then after a period of courtship,
Just after the river had "riz,"
They were bound in the bonds of marriage
And her name was changed to his.
This home was blessed with a baby boy,
On the first anniversary day.
This small, newborn son was named Roy,
Just the reason, I cannot say.

This family of three went back to the East
Where the doctor could go to school.
He must study hard to hold the lead
In order the sickness to rule.

It was there that the second boy was born,
The name Floyd was given to him.
This second son was short and fat,
By no means could you call him slim.

Then, after school they returned to Grand,
That is where he had started to work.
A few people only, lived on this land,
But none were known to shirk.

So on they stayed in this little town
Where the people and friends were true,
Where things never changed, from time to time
And the skies were always blue.

Then came the third little baby boy,
Not a stitch was on his back.
Haskell was the real name he got,
But everyone calls him Hack.
Then they moved away from Grand,
It was far too small a town;
Shattuck was only a few miles away
And now, that is where he is found.

In this new town, he worked as hard
As any one man ever did.
He kept to his studies first of all,
A habit since only a kid.
Each year he went back East to school,
He kept right up to date;
To study hard is his principal rule
To be idle spells out fate.

All this study is personal gain;
This, he knows in full,
Although some days it was dark as rain,
But he did not wait for pull.
But now it pays to specialize,
So the doctor took his place;
Better surgeons do not live
In the realm of the human race.

Operations must be done,
They help to stop the pain.
All his patients go home well,
And feeling fine again.

Now his practice is too big
For just one man to do,
He works from dawn to setting sun,
And then, works all night through.

He just can't find a time to rest,
He answers every call
From operations that are bad
To babies that simply bawl.

He has worked for every dollar,
That has found its way to him.
He can now enjoy some comfort,
Though collections oft are dim.

For the many years of service
That he always gladly gave
He has never left a crevice,
He has always strived to save.
His home for long was moderate,
It stood on common loam;
But after many years of toil,
He built a modern home.

His comfort now is well defined,
His home is now complete;
Once more, his mind can be at rest
Though he still retains his seat.
Lo, the little rest could not last long,
Hospital needs grow still,
So here comes another building,
And here comes another bill!

The hospital is now complete,
And all is well again,
But yet his mind is working fast,
As it has always been.
The three sons of Dr. Newman
Are still attending school;
They want to be good doctors,
As their father made the rule.

Now, Dr. Newman has a dream,
He wants three doctors, too!
And, though far off, the ideal seems,
Let's hope his dream comes true.

Dr. Floyd S. Newman
(Written while a student)

I remember, while I was attending grade school, Dad bought his first microscope. I doubt if he had ever had instruction in its use, but he did realize its value and spent many hours mastering it. Soon after he purchased the instrument, he found a specimen containing TB germs. The slide was kept under the scope for several days and he proudly demonstrated it to many who came to his office. He also showed it to me, describing it to me very carefully, so he could be sure that I, too, saw the germs.

Not long afterward, he obtained his first X-ray equipment. By present standards it was very limited in its use, but at the time, it was the finest piece of equipment a doctor could own. Again, he took a great deal of pride in showing it off with both the pictures he had taken and the use of the fluoroscope.

I remember him saying many times that his main ambition for us was the best possible education, but he would not try to influence us in the matter of a profession. I am sure he kept his word. But, by his way of life, his philosophy and his success, we felt that there was no other work, trade or profession quite as good as medicine.

Our first trip home, after entering medical school, was not with good news. We all insisted we had worked hard, but were afraid of failure when the grades were tallied. He assured us that, in that event, we could always try again. Soon afterward, he visited us in school to learn for himself if things were as bad as we feared.

I was happy and proud to introduce him to my class and my instructors, but feared his visit to the dean. However, that evening, I took him to the dean's office, then waited outside in the hall for him to come out and give me the bad news. To my surprise, he came out smiling. "What makes you boys think you are failing?" he said. "The dean says you are all well above the middle of the class." This was news to us since the school never gave out grades until just before finals, but realizing the many questions we had missed, we expected the worst.

Dad's pride showed all over. He invited the whole fraternity down to the restaurant for dinner. Each year after this, he visited us some time during the term, and attended our classes. He studied with us, took part in sessions with other students and always took us out to meals while he was there. Some of the other students looked forward to his visits almost as much as we.

After graduation, he made us welcome if we wished to join him in practice. Nobody ever had a better opening; our association with him professionally was as much a part of our training as our schooling. He insisted we work as a unit rather than as individuals and we have followed this plan successfully.

However, the first few months of our practice in Shattuck was disappointing to us boys. Dr. O. C. had all the practice! The people he had served for so long were not at all inclined to change doctors. I have known people to wait three and four hours for him to give them a "cold shot." They allowed us to take care of them only under his close direction. He made every effort to refer patients to us, but with little success. It was not until we got more training in our different specialties that we began to get patients of our own. Then, the total number of patients seen in the clinic began to show an increase.

As long as he was able, Dad retained the lead. He was quick to accept the new, as soon as he was

178 . . .

convinced it had merit; he was quick to recommend a change when he felt it was needed; he was quick to note when there was evidence of neglect. He worked hard, was thorough and expected others to do the same. It was this drive that spelled his success.

Yes, we are proud of our father and we feel that our clinic, our hospital and our town are a memorial to him.

Dr. Floyd S. Newman

The following cannot relate my many experiences with my father, although I knew him not well enough until I became associated with him in a business way. The former statement I make with regret, both on his part and mine, though the regret is softened when I realize that he belonged, not to just a few, but to the many. His creed, his code of ethics made it a necessity to place his patients

M. H. Newman, M.D.

and their needs before association with his family, desirable as that would have been. For this reason, my home corrections were made by my mother and very few final decisions as to my activities were made by my father. His advice and consultation was always sound and stern to me.

One of the most outstanding memories of persistence on his part was that his children obtain sufficient education to qualify them to be self-supporting. In our home, in the early periods when a college education was not considered a necessity either to financial or mental satisfaction, schooling was a progressive thing, the grade school to be followed by high school, and without break, the college education to follow. If one could not finance the college courses one wanted, then it followed that one could work for them. The latter was not necessary in our case and although the majority of my classmates with whom I graduated from high school did not proceed to higher education, my father's code was so instilled in my thinking, that I did not consider ceasing the quest for knowledge. He did not advise me to take up medicine and to my knowledge, did not advise my brothers to do so, but encouraged us along lines in which we were most interested.

My deepest impression of his affection for his family occurred when we three sons were going to school in Texas, one at Baylor Medical School in Dallas, the other two at Baylor University, an academic school in Waco. We decided to remain together at Dallas during the Christmas holidays and save Dad the expense of our traveling home. On Christmas morning, Dad called us long-distance, asking us to disregard the expense and come home.

Dad enjoyed the realization of a dream on July 29, 1932 when my wife, Cornelia presented him with a grand daughter, JoAnn. He had always said that it was his regret that he did not have a daughter and was partial to girl babies. Haskell, jr., born on March 29, 1937 was his first grandson, and though he never showed any partiality, still anyone could see that JoAnn was the "apple of his eye."

I can say that Dad was a master teacher, not only in the professional way, but in the teaching of morals, by word and action. Strict honesty was his motto, and condemnation was not one of his traits. "It can't be done" was not in his phraseology; the strength of that attitude ruled when we built the clinic, it reigned in his, and our, yearly attendance of more organized medical classes and clinics; he maintained the belief that education had always just started. That we should all give his people of northwest Oklahoma the best possible care, both diagnostically and in treatment, was a religion to my father.

His sincerety was expressed not only in his tone of voice, but by his facial expressions as well as his gait. He was never satisfied with anything short of perfection in medicine and surgery.

To say he was a genius would, in my estimation, be correct. He had no photographic mind but his persistence and long thought, or the observation of details, helped him to become great. He had a research type of outlook in his thoughts, not attempting to achieve greatness, but only to be of service.

Dr. M. Haskell Newman

CHAPTER XIII

TOUCH OF HONOR

The latter decade and a half of Doctor's life brought recognition and reward, most of which was unsought and totally unexpected by this unassuming personality. His fame as a physician and surgeon had spread over a large area, and his hospital and clinic was truly the "Little Mayo of the West." Not only was the man a great doctor, but a humanitarian second to none of his day.

One afternoon in 1939, the telephone in Doctor's private office rang and he was summoned from a routine check-up of a patient.

"Long distance from Oklahoma City, Doctor," the nurse said.

"Hello, Dr. Newman," said a booming voice on the wire. "This is Governor Phillips. Just wanted to tell you that I have appointed you to the State Board of Medical Examiners. Any objection, sir?"

"That's a job for big shots, isn't it, Governor? Well, I'm no big shot. I'm just a country doctor."

"Red" Phillips laughed heartily, then his voice grew serious. "The doctors of this city and over the state have a deep respect for your integrity and your unsurpassed medical knowledge and skill. The practitioners of Oklahoma would be honored to have you on the Board."

In the fall of 1939, in Philadelphia, Doctor received a Fellowship in the American College of Surgeons, an honor bestowed later on his son, Haskell. As an instructor of medicine, Doctor was recognized as outstanding.

Further appointments as Examiner on the state medical Board were given him by Governors Robert S. Kerr in 1943, by Roy J. Turner in 1947 and again by Johnston Murray near the end of Doctor's life. Dr. Haskell was appointed to fill his unexpired term.

He was a life member of the Oklahoma Historical Society and wrote his brief "Reminiscences" for the official quarterly publication, the **Chronicles of Oklahoma.** In addition, O. H. Richards wrote a paper about his old friend for the **Chronicles.** The Oklahoma Memorial Association, of which he was twice president, became increasingly aware of the life and works of this country doctor, and its board of directors chose Dr. Newman to be inducted into the state Hall of Fame on November 16, 1943.

A life size portrait in oil was ordered by the Memorial group, to be placed in the Oklahoma Historical Society building in Oklahoma City, and the renowned artist, Dr. Joseph de Sigall, of Tulsa was commissioned to paint the portrait. The artist and the newspaper people in Tulsa were particularly impressed by Doctor's homespun personality. One referred to him as "an erect, sparkling, kindly-eyed little man."

A reporter wrote: "Doctor Newman, legend has it, is the nucleus of Shattuck. 'Doc came first,' grin his cronies. 'The hotels and business houses came to take care of his patients and the town just grew.' " Of Doctor, the artist said: "The whole town is built around him. He takes maybe a chicken in payment from the poor. Thirty thousand people come to his hospital a year."

That their doctor was to be so honored was a keen delight to the people of Shattuck and they went all out for a community "Doctor Newman Day" on Sunday before his induction on November 16. Once more, friends filled the high school auditorium, and to Doctor's intense pleasure, old Day countains again occupied a reserved section. The program reflected thinking of the day; the time was during war.

The high school band played the Star Spangled Banner after the flag salute and Rev. Thacker gave the invocation. The chorus sang "When the Lights Go On Again Over the World" and JoAnn Newman honored her grandfather with one of his favorite selections in a piano solo. Clinton Johnston, president of the Chamber of Commerce gave an address, followed by Judge Ben Barnett, a political protege of Dr. Newman. Mrs. E. J. Rader, Sorosis club prexy presented Doctor, and many tears were mixed with the thunderous applause. Again, the chorus sang one of Doctor's favorites, "Home on the Range" and Rev. Chambers gave the benediction.

That following Tuesday, one hundred thirty townspeople from Shattuck made the trip over to Oklahoma City for the induction cermonies at the Biltmore Hotel. The banquet room was filled, and Shattuckians overflowed onto the stage. Because rarely had anyone present seen such a comparative turnout, the friends and townspeople were asked to stand. In the ceremonies, General W. S. Key accepted the portrait from the artist for hanging in the Hall of Fame.

Doctor, though enjoying the occasion and particularly the evidence of love from his friends, nevertheless remarked at the close: "Well, now that I've been hanged, I'm ready to get back home."

One of the most appreciated gestures Doctor ever acknowledged was a poem written by Judge O. E. Enfield on the occasion of the dedication of the hospital and clinic in 1937:

Behold ye now assembled here,
What see ye to admire?
A frame of concrete and of steel
Cased in brick once tried in fire?
What see ye? Smooth and polished floors,
High ceilings wide of span?
See ye these material things,
 And not the man?

What see ye here? A plat of ground?
Some shrubbery and some trees?
Ah, in the background, those who think
See greater things than these;
Yea, in the background there was Hope
When young manhood began,
Toil, Faith and Patience prove the worth
 Of him, the man.

What see ye here: these instruments
By worthy science wrought?
Still, when in need of surgery
Do they not count for naught,
Except for skill of hand and heart
To execute a plan?
Why place your life so in the care
 Of him, the man?

Do ye with wonder view the house?
The ornamented walls?
Do ye admire the furnishings?
The cool and spacious halls?

Well, greater things than these are here:
Look ye, behold who can,
The honor and integrity
    Of him, the man.

Or will ye say the man is rich?
Or will ye call him great
Because he labored through long years
Incessantly and late?
Your estimate is incomplete
For by his side, I scan
A helpmeet true, the faithful wife
    Of him, the man.

Nor is that all there is to see,
There is some credit due
To white-capped, patient, trusted nurse,
On duty all night through.
Shall we not praise them, each and all
Who served him as time ran?
To give them credit can't detract
    From him, the man.

Long live this institution!
When its founder's course is run,
May the honor of the father
Then actuate the son:
With water fill the goblet
And while peal the pipes of Pan,
We'll drink the health of Each and All
    Who labored with the man.

In 1947, Doctor was voted the most outstanding physician in Oklahoma by state members of the medical profession, an honor greatly cherished by members of his family. A. M. Chitty, secretary of the Alumni Association of Sewanee's University of the South stated at that time that, with all of Dr. Newman's sons associated with him in medicine, it was the most unusual record in the files of that institution. In addition to other affiliations and honors, Doctor had become, by now, a trustee of the Oklahoma Medical Research group.

As the younger doctors were able to assume more of the practice, Doctor began to take a bit of his well-earned ease, but did not actually retire until April, 1952. That year, in the sunset of his days, was a glorious time for Doctor. His was a

Doctor and Mrs. Newman on the occasion of their Golden Wedding Anniversary, September 18, 1952.

188 . . .

full and complete life, a dedicated life which he had crowned with his professed faith and belief in an even better life to come. That last full year, in 1952, Doctor received his fifty-year pin in Masonry and his half-century citation from the Oklahoma Medical Association.

On September 18, he and his beloved Della observed their golden wedding anniversary, in remembrance of the marriage back in Old Grand. Once more, friends of that early day who were living, came to pay their honor.

It would seem that the Great Physician himself blessed the several anniversary events of that year to Doctor's own liking, as the final glory of a good life.

His was a full and complete life. That last full year, in 1952, Doctor received his fifty-year pin in Masonry and his half-century citation from the Oklahoma Medical Association. Here, left to right are Cecil J. Nash, Dr. O. C. Newman, W. K. Suthers, O. H. Richards and T. N. Young

Doctor had done all the good he could do for humanity. He loved them, one and all, and they loved him in return. A faint smile flickered across his face, there on the pillow. Outside his bedroom window, the stirrings of spring spoke of new life. It was just such a morning when he first came to old Grand. It was just such a morning when he met his lovely Della. Over at the hospital, his staff was busy restoring life and health to his people. They would carry on the work he had begun, and he was satisfied. It was good to be at home, with his loved ones near. It was good to be home—

* * *

Oscar Clarence Newman, M.D. died at his home at 10:30 on Saturday morning, March 14, 1953. Services were held in the First Baptist church of Shattuck, and throngs of people filed past mountains of flowers to pay their last respects to a soldier among men, the humanitarian and friend. And Doctor was laid to rest in the friendly sod of the Panhandle country which he loved.

> *"—All through the prairie countries and out across the plains to the passes of the Rockies there are people who have reason to bless the name of Dr. Newman."*

THE END.

ACKNOWLEDGMENTS

Q. A. (Quin) Walck
Arthur Ben Chitty
Dr. Marcus O. Shivers
Dr. S. B. Leslie
Dr. Everett S. Lain
Muriel H. Wright
O. H. Richards
Charlotte Kuntz
O. Fant Word
F. Hiner Dale
Charles A. Evans
Solon Porter
Bob Denny
Mrs. Frank Kolander
Mrs. Harold McIntosh
Mrs. Fred Thierstein
Murl Travis
Daisy Thorne Gilbert
Mozelle Allison Jackson
Mrs. J. G. Richards
A. E. Williams
Sam A. McKeel, M.D.
Peggy Wallen
Gladys Klepper
Edwin Jackson
Henry A. Adams
Rev. Dan N. Curb
G. L. Johnson, M.D.
Anzley Ellis
Mrs. C. O. Mangold
C. C. Colbert
Mrs. J. R. Reed
James M. Tuthill
Mrs. Mary Wilson
Cecil E. Henson
Mrs. Mabel Moore
A. J. Lahann

Rudolph Trieber
Ray C. Ingle
E. H. Snyder, M.D.
Mrs. J. D. Reisig
Clavance C. Clark
Mr. and Mrs. George Foster
George Gantz
Dr. J. J. Davis
Robert S. Kerr
Mrs. Anna B. Korn
Leo Meier
Frank W. Patterson
John Barcafer
W. K. Suthers
Opal Booth Karn, R.N.
M. Louise Cramer, R.N.
Goldie Wilson Hunter
Naomi Dalrymple Meier
Mr. and Mrs. Rolf O. Brown
A. L. Buell, M.D.
Paul C. Christian, M.D.
Porter Brown, M.D.
James Stevenson, M.D.
Tom Lowry, M.D.
G. F. Matthews, M.D.
Earl D. McBride, M.D.
James D. Osborn, M.D.
Mrs. George H. Suthers
Mrs. Dave Johnson
Rev. Lewis M. Hancock
Rev. C. Chalon Meadows
Rev. Robert R. Chambers
Mrs. Joseph (Dock) Smith
Wilmer E. Grindstaff, D.D.
Norma E. Kolander, M.T.
Drs. John and Stella Davis
Nellie Hersh Kinderdick

Charles C. Tener
E. E. Shirley
Dr. Joseph de Sigall
Raymond Laughlin
Mrs. Cecil Nash
Mrs. Walter Deickman
Rev. J. G. Holder
Milroy Karn

Virginia Pior Bavensfeld
S. W. Northup
Junnie B. Williams
Austa Parker Gilson
Lorena Cordell
Edwina Cordell, R.N.
Josephine Thomas

CPSIA information can be obtained
at www.ICGtesting.com
Printed in the USA
LVOW13s2318020317

526015LV00031B/633/P

9 781258 419783